Road to Ground Zero

Finding God's Will

Fred Bishop
As Told to Shane Bishop
and Roger Lipe

© Copyright 1993 — Fred Bishop

All rights reserved. This book is protected under the copyright laws of the United States of America. This book may not be copied or reprinted for commercial gain or profit. Short quotations or occasional page copying for personal or group study is permitted and encouraged. Permission will be granted upon request. Unless otherwise identified, Scripture quotations are from The King James Version of the Bible.

Take note that the name satan and related names are not capitalized. We choose not to acknowledge him, even to the point of violating grammatical rules.

Treasure House
a division of
Destiny Image
P.O. Box 310
Shippensburg, PA 17257-0310

ISBN 1-56043-755-3

For Worldwide Distribution
Printed in the U.S.A.

Destiny Image books are available through these fine distributors outside the United States:

Christian Growth, Inc.,
Jalan Kilang-Timor, Singapore 0315

Lifestream
Nottingham, England

Rhema Ministries Trading
Randburg, South Africa

Salvation Book Centre
Petaling, Jaya, Malaysia

Successful Christian Living
Capetown, Rep. of South Africa

Vision Resources
Ponsonby, Auckland, New Zealand

WA Buchanan Company
Geebung, Queensland, Australia

Word Alive
Niverville, Manitoba, Canada

Contents

	Foreword	v
	Introduction	ix
Chapter I	A Place in This World	1
Chapter II	Buffalo, Rebels, and Cowboys	13
Chapter III	Baptized With Struggle	25
Chapter IV	Nonconventional God	39
Chapter V	A Giant Step on the Road	53
Chapter VI	The Color of Ministry	67
Chapter VII	Living by Faith?	77
Chapter VIII	Singing in the Attic	85
Chapter IX	So Proud of God	99
Chapter X	Conclusion: No Greater Love	113

Foreword

Contained in the pages of this book is a model for finding one's ultimate place in service of the Lord Jesus. The principles illustrated herein are sometimes very obvious; at other times they are quite different from anything you may have been taught.

At the core of this project is the concept that, as we grow in Christ and look for a place of ministry, we must allow for the process to include hard work, humble servitude and a good measure of pain. The process is neither quick nor pleasant, as God is more concerned with our character in ministry than He is with our gifts, abilities or depth of knowledge for the ministry.

The subject addressed here is the process—the refining, shaping and hammering of a person's character into the form required for God's most effective use of the minister. *The Road to Ground Zero* is about the trip, not the destination.

Most of us rightly set our sights on the goal of finding our ultimate place in ministry, but we often despise the means that God is using to prepare us for that ministry. It is the years of study, the months of seemingly wasted effort and the periods of despair at losing sight of the goal that mold our character into a usable form.

As a vehicle for making these principles understood and in order to illustrate their use we are employing a set of stories from the life of the Rev. Fred L. Bishop, president of No Greater Love Ministries of DuQuoin, Illinois.

These are brief glimpses of God's handiwork in Fred's life. Some of the material is quite humorous and lighthearted, while other parts are filled with suspense and danger.

This is not an autobiography in the strictest sense, rather it is a testimony to the faithfulness of God as witnessed by a man who dared to pursue the Lord Jesus with reckless abandon. *Rather than tell you the story of "one who embodied God's will," we will tell you stories of "one who employed God's will."*

The Road to Ground Zero is not intended to gather a following for a man or his ministry, but to inspire a commitment to the Living God and the call He has made upon each one of us. May the pages that follow be used by the Holy Spirit of Christ to deepen your devotion and to strengthen your resolve to arrive at your own *ground zero,* the place of beginning.

Shane L. Bishop and Roger D. Lipe

Introduction

There is a type of bomb that does not detonate until it strikes the ground. The exact spot at which the bomb impacts the earth and explodes is called "ground zero." The explosion which starts at ground zero has widespread effects from the shock waves produced. Its power is felt at great distances and over a long period of time. Christians long to see their lives harness the kind of power that affects others far beyond the point at which they stand. Most Christians never find their way to *ground zero*. Despite grand visions and callings, most die before ever arriving at the place where they make a real impact on the world.

We all want our lives to have shock-wave-like effects, reaching people in ever-increasing circles of influence for Christ's Kingdom. However, no one can begin effective and lasting work without reaching a *ground zero*. Whether you're a minister struggling to make an impact on your community, a committed layman working in your church or simply a believer trying to honor Christ with your everyday life, you must pay the price to arrive at the starting point. *Ground zero* is an exciting place to be, but the road to it is narrow and difficult.

I reached my *ground zero* in 1975 in the Austrian Alps. Our Bible-smuggling team had narrowly escaped from Bratislava, Czechoslovakia, and I could scarcely believe we were alive. I was lying on the very mountains on which *The Sound of Music* had been filmed. I was meditating on the scripture that says, "The angel of the Lord encamps around those who fear Him, and He delivers them—again and again" (see Psalm 34:7). I was wondering how many "agains" there could be for me. How many more times would I have to write out my will before the end would come? My nerves were shattered; even the tranquil beauty of the mountains of Salzburg, Austria, could offer no solace. My one desire was that God's peace would come back to my emotions, my spirit and my body. I was waiting before God and listening with an attentivness that only a person in my condition could muster. Suddenly my spirit sensed that something special was about to take place. I thought I had once again laid down my life in God's service and felt I was waiting for His commendation. Instead of an award, I was given a commission that ultimately became my *ground zero*. God spoke these words to my heart:

You have served me faithfully, you have laid down your life, and I am pleased. However, your life is no longer contagious to my Body; instead you have become a spectacle, and your new commission will change that. You have trusted Me, you have followed Me, you have been a part of great and mighty exploits, but now you must die.

I thought at first that it meant that my life was over, but then God gave me the verse, "...Except a grain of wheat falls into the ground and dies, it will never reproduce..." (see John 12:24). I heard God saying:

Now I will take you back home to the land of your fathers and cause you to be used to help others experience Me. I will use your life to call forth laborers into My harvest. You will see people in churches, all kinds of churches, who have a desire to serve Me, and you will be able to ask them in accordance with My Word, "Why are you standing here at noonday?" And they will answer, "Because no one has hired me." *I will use you to put the gospel into the hands of faithful men.* They will be raised up and begin many ministries and reach throughout the world.

Little did I realize at the time that my apprenticeship was over, my *ground zero* had arrived, and my new life in Christ had begun.

Along the way to *ground zero* I had learned many important principles which would be foundational for the ministry. These principles also are the key themes for this book. Among those most notable are the following:

- The value of formal education.

- The concept of being an apprentice, a journeyman and then a craftsman.

- "A man's gift makes room for him..." (Prov. 18:16; NKJV).

- We must remain true to the calling which God has placed upon us.

- When God speaks, obey.

- When we're moving in God's plan, He will provide signs and wonders to confirm His Word.

In the following chapters you will find living illustrations of the above concepts and gain a feeling for the cost of learning them. My prayer for you is not that you will be immediately transported to *ground zero,* but that God will not let you arrive until you are fully ready.

Chapter I

A Place in This World

Sunfield, Illinois, has never been an exciting place. Throughout the duration of my boyhood, I do not recall anyone coming to Sunfield for an exciting vacation. The community formed around an underground coal mine in the first part of this century. Miners moved into the tiny area, located three miles north of DuQuoin on Highway 51, looking for opportunity. What most of them got was a subsistence level of living and a big tab at the Bailey Brothers' General Store. By the time Frederick Laverne Bishop was born on September 12, 1939, the mining boom had gone bust. Our family eventually bought some farm land that sat over the underground mines. The folks who stayed in Sunfield eventually got jobs at other mines or became farmers. Soon three families dominated the population of the community, the Baileys, the Vancils and the Bishops.

I was Hal and Inez Bishop's only son, and they probably figured I would be the one to carry the family farm into the next generation. As I reached high school our family worked a 176-acre farm that grew crops, had an orchard and raised sheep, cows, hogs and chickens. My sisters, Halene, Donna and Sue, and I all had to work very hard to keep the farm productive. I remember sitting on the tractor plowing and watching the cars rolling along the highway. I always wondered where they were going and if, someday, I would go somewhere, too.

At the age of 14 I was startled by a dream in the middle of a summer night; it left me wide-awake in my bed. I could see Jesus on a cloud; He was coming to take His people to Heaven. Many of the people ahead of me were going up into the cloud, but not everyone. As the cloud got closer to me I suddenly became afraid. Would I be taken up with Christ, or would I be left behind? When the cloud was right in front of me I awakened in a cold sweat and convulsed into an upright position.

For the next several months I thought about my dream and determined to discover what it took to go to Heaven. Word around Sunfield was that only good people went to Heaven, but I wondered how God decided who was good and who was bad. A sermon was preached in church one Sunday about the second coming of Christ. The Rev. Glen Fisher said, "One person will be taken, and the other left behind." The message got through to me! I made a conscious decision to hang around with the worst sort of people available. This way, if Jesus returned I would surely be taken ahead of them. Even as a young teenager this solution didn't make much sense, but it was all I had to go on.

Later that year at the annual revival at the Sunfield Methodist Church, a sermon was preached that brought me to my knees. The minister answered my question, "What must I do to be saved?" and at the altar of that small church my sister Sue and I gave our hearts to Jesus Christ. From that day until the present I have never doubted my salvation. Junior Axley was the church's youth leader, and he encouraged me to get more involved in the church. He could sense I had a love for God and a desire to know more about Him, but he really didn't know how to help me. It felt good to know I was going to Heaven for my next life, but I was beginning to wonder what I was going to do with this one.

In the summer of my 16th year opportunity came along for me to attend the Methodist Youth Camp in Eldorado, Illinois. I hesitantly asked Dad if I could attend, and when he saw what it meant to me he said I could go if all the farming was done. When camp time came there was excitement in my soul. This was the chance I had been waiting for, and I really hoped God would call me into the ministry. Few young people have ever attended a camp with so much at stake.

At the camp I met an exceptional, older gentleman by the name of Brother Tommy Harper. Brother Harper loved God so much that it literally radiated from within him. He had something about him that I was looking for. He participated in an optional, early morning prayer meeting, and I didn't miss a single one. The folks at the prayer meeting had an odd way of praying which I had never encountered before; they all prayed out loud at the same time. It was bothersome at first, but I finally decided that God could hear every prayer being spoken, so I joined right in. On the final night of the camp I went up to the altar during the invitation, but was severely disappointed that no one came to talk with me. Bitterly disappointed I concluded that camp was a sort of one-week fantasy world where everyone was supposed to have a great time and then go home and live happily ever after. It didn't work out that way for me.

I graduated from DuQuoin High School in 1957 with an agricultural scholarship to attend the University of Illinois. I left the security of home for the first time and did not do well adjusting to the outside world. College was frustrating, because I became increasingly aware that I didn't want to be a farmer. The only thing I had going right in my life was my health, and it was turning sour fast. After making it through 12 years of school without missing a single day I began to miss a lot of classes due to my health. I was hospitalized during two of my three semesters at the university. To add insult to injury, my spiritual quest seemed to be going nowhere. Every Sunday I would attend a different Methodist church, but could never find peace within myself. After a few months I had visited every Methodist church in Champaign and Urbana and still could not find spiritual fulfillment or any direction for my life.

During that time I was dating a very nice Catholic girl from DuQuoin. She suggested that the Catholic church might offer some answers to the questions I was pondering, so I consented to receive instruction in the Roman Catholic church at Champaign. The priest had many good ideas, and he seemed to have a love for God, but the entire experience was disturbing to my spirit. During a question time I asked the priest to explain the concept of purgatory. He said, "God forgives our sins, but we must still make them right, regardless of how sorry we are for them." I had discovered the reason I could not become a Catholic! No amount of purgatory could ever erase my sins. I knew that Jesus Christ was the only One who could wash away sin! The price for my salvation had already been paid on Calvary. When he had finished his explanation I inquired as to whether he was going to go to purgatory. He grinned, exposing his bright buck teeth, and said, "Just long enough to say hi to all the boys."

After saying farewell to Catholicism I looked for direction in another area. I went and tested for vocational aptitude. The test showed the only two things I was interested in were religion and speech. The psychologist may have thought it obvious I would become a minister, but at the time I didn't even know where to start.

In 1958 I was hospitalized in Champaign with a diagnosis of a bad case of the flu. I was reading the Bible in my hospital room one day when a Christian nurse began conversing with me. In the course of our conversation she saw the picture of my girlfriend and asked, "Is your girlfriend a Christian?" I honestly replied that I didn't know. She flippantly said, "Then you can't marry her," and stormed out of the room. I was furious with her. I thought, "What's it to you, lady?" The next day she brought in a scripture explaining her position. She read, "Be not unequally yoked together with unbelievers" (II Cor. 6:14, KJV). "Are you going to obey God or not?" On my next break from college I broke up with my Catholic girlfriend, and we never dated again.

I spent the following summer at home farming. One evening I decided to go skating at the DuQuoin "Triple L" Skating Rink after church. There was a 16-year-old girl there who caught my eye, named Jan Burton, from nearby Tamaroa. She was with a girlfriend, and was chaperoned by her mother, Helen.

> I had gone to the skating rink that night with my mom and a girlfriend. We loved to roller skate, and on this night I had on a brand-new, white skirt and blouse to accent my white skates. I had

been praying for a Christian boyfriend for some time and had heard that Fred Bishop was a Christian. He was also very handsome. Later in the evening Fred asked me to skate with him. When I said yes he practically pulled my arm out of the socket dragging me into the rink. He was trying to show off by skating fast and caused our skates to get tangled up, and we both fell headlong on the floor.

At the end of the evening Fred asked my mom if he could take me home. I was excited until I saw his car. It was an old, rusted-out farm vehicle, and when I got in I could see the road through the floorboard. Fred drove like he skated, fast. Rather than use the highway, he took me home over ten miles of dirt roads. As we rode I could see grey clouds of dust rolling up through the floorboard and settling on my new, white skating outfit. By the time I got home I was filthy, but I had met someone very special.

Jan Bishop

I did everything imaginable to impress Jan that night, from my college lingo to superfast skating. I soon found Jan wasn't looking for a boyfriend who could show off, she was looking for someone who loved God. We began to date that summer and spent much of our time in church. Sunfield Methodist had Thursday midweek services, and her church, Holt's Prairie Baptist, had services on Wednesday. We went to her church Sunday morning and mine Sunday afternoon, only to return to her church for evening services. That whole summer we attended five services a week. No one had to tell me that this beautiful blonde from Tamaroa was the girl for me.

The fall after Jan and I started dating was a period of intense struggle and reevaluation in my life. It was true I had found the girl I had prayed for, but there still were many unresolved questions concerning my life's direction. Since my health problems were continuing, I reentered the hospital and was given a diagnosis of rheumatoid arthritis, a stress-induced form of arthritis that stiffens the joints. I dropped out of the University of Illinois. Back in Sunfield and away from the stress and strain of college, one might think my condition would have improved, but it continued to get worse. My joints soon reached the point at which they were so stiff I had trouble getting out of bed some mornings. One day I was lying on my bed and praying about my situation. I was sick and tired of being sick and tired, and I honestly believed that God could heal me. In my spirit I heard God tell me to get up and run if I wanted to be healed. Deliberately and with great pain, I rose from my bed and slowly put on my shoes. Stumbling out the back door I began to walk, then to run. I ran slowly at first, but gradually increased speed. With each step, it felt like my insides were coming out, but on I ran. After running up our half-mile lane, I turned east toward the DuQuoin Lake and continued running. This was a once-and-for-all showdown with this thing, and only one of us was going to win!

What a sight it must have been to see an exhausted young man running down a country road in such obvious pain that he was doubled over. With each step, however, the pain lessened, and the joints loosened. Soon I was running stronger than I ever had run before! The arthritis "popped off" my body like buttons off a tight shirt that day, and I have never been bothered by rheumatoid arthritis since. God had healed me and taught me a valuable lesson by which I continued to live: when I hear God, I obey, no matter how unlikely the command. Looking back to that difficult time it is obvious I had my first face-off with the devil. It would not be the last.

I married Janice Jean Burton at Holt's Prairie Baptist Church on June 12, 1959. After the wedding we moved to Wood River, Illinois, where I worked in the steel mill in nearby Alton.

The following year we moved near Chicago to find our place in the world. We settled in a small town called Sandwich in De Kalb County. I got a job at an office furniture factory in Aurora and struggled to bring some stability to our lives. One Sunday we visited an outstanding little church in nearby Somonauk, called Somonauk Baptist. The pastor was an energetic and talented young man named Gerald Winkleman. When we walked into the sanctuary we were met by an usher, who asked where I worked and gathered some information about us. He wisely took us to sit by a man who also worked at the factory, and it didn't take us very long to feel accepted as a part of their church. We experienced such love and growth there that we became involved in the various church ministries. I began to go with church ministry teams to the rescue mission in Aurora.

It was just when things were seemingly coming together that we received news that my father had died. My nerves carried me into the pits of depression. Soon I could no longer work and would sit for hours in the backyard in a chair. We needed a vacation!

Where do you go when life is coming apart at the seams? You go back home. Once in Sunfield, I was appointed to do all the odd jobs other family members did not have time to do. The anticipated time of relaxation and reflection did not materialize. We promptly left for my mother-in-law's house in Jacksonville, Illinois. We were driving up Route 13 when our aqua Plymouth convertible's motor began to miss. Not being mechanically inclined, I prayed before getting out of the car, "Father, if You will help me to fix this car, I will not leave Jacksonville until I have heard from You." When I looked under the hood, even I could see that one of the spark plug wires was unattached! I excitedly connected the plug wire, and we went on to Jacksonville. I was so proud of God!

At the home of my mother-in-law, Helen, I had a vision during the night. Three warm rays of sunlight streamed down from Heaven and rested upon me. But what could it mean? God showed me that one ray was Junior Axley, who had been my youth leader when I was a teenager. The second ray was the Reverend Glen Fisher, my pastor in my teen years at Sunfield Methodist Church. The remaining ray represented Jan. God instructed me that just as these three special people had reflected God's light to me, I was to reflect His light to others. The church held a missions conference later in the year, and during the invitation Jan and I went forward to accept our call into missions. God's plan for us was beginning to make sense.

On April 2, 1962, Jan gave birth to a red-headed, nine-pound boy we named Shane Lavern Bishop. We named him for the western movie, *Shane*, we recently had seen starring Alan Ladd. Laverne was a family name that I passed down the line to my son. Dad was named Hallan Laverne, I was Frederick Laverne, and so the name lived on. I'm not sure why we dropped the "e" in the spelling. When Shane was in junior high the situation comedy, *Lavern and Shirley*, popularized Lavern as a girl's name, and I'm not sure Shane has ever forgiven me for his middle name! Recently Shane has reclaimed the name and goes by the Rev. Shane Lavern Bishop. When his son was born in 1984 he broke the family tradition by naming him Zechariah Christian Bishop. He said he just couldn't give the name Lavern to an innocent child!

Accepting God's calling began a whole new chapter in our lives, but we really had no idea how to pursue the call. We began to consult with our pastor, the Rev. Winkleman, and it became obvious that if we wanted to go into ministry we would have to go back to college. Many people think school is not necessary if an individual has a call to ministry, but I have seen many churches and ministries fouled up, because their leaders did not know the things that they would have learned in school. The Rev. Winkleman advised us to go to a Bible college and soon announced he would be leaving the church to become a professor at the Buffalo Bible Institute in Buffalo, New York. After looking at the program for the school we decided to move to Buffalo and attend in the fall. We sold our house trailer and our convertible and excitedly left Illinois to follow our hearts to Buffalo.

Chapter II

Buffalo, Rebels, and Cowboys

God had called us into the ministry, and we decided a formal Christian education was the best way for us to prepare for God's call. We arrived in Buffalo in August of 1962. We were bright eyed and bushy tailed, ready to attend the Buffalo Bible Institute. Within 30 days after our move everything went wrong. We were involved in a serious automobile accident in Orchard Park that totaled our only car. The impact sent Jan's head through the windshield, broke Shane's arm and injured my back. My back was hurt so badly that I couldn't work for some time. Reality scoffed at our youthful visions of grandeur, and our balloon popped in a hurry. There we were, half a continent from home, no car, no income, no job and all of us injured. Most people think that when God calls one to make a major move that He will make his life smooth and easy. It was not so for us.

In those difficult times, God became intensely real to us. We could identify with David, who found that "It was good for me that I have been afflicted...", for in his afflictions he cried out to God, and He heard him and delivered him (see Ps. 119:71). In Buffalo we found no matter how bad things got God was always more than sufficient to take care of our needs. We were living in a three-room, unfurnished apartment. Jan and I slept every night on a rug, and Shane slept on an old baby mattress placed on the floor. Jan celebrated her 21st birthday in that small apartment with no furniture; it wasn't much of a party. For recreation during the winter, to pass the endless hours, Jan would go out to the garage and play an old piano which was being stored there. Bundled up and wearing gloves she would sit for hours and play that old upright in the frigid Buffalo winter.

> We knew when we went to Buffalo we would have to live by faith. There was really no way we could get Fred through school and support a family. We would try to sleep late, because we knew we could only afford to eat two meals a day. With the wreck, we hit the bottom, but after that everything really seemed to get better. Our insurance settlement came through, and Fred was off to a good start in school.
>
> I was lonely. Shane and I would be in the apartment all day, every day, while Fred went to work and school. Fred was elected Valentine King of

the Bible Institute, and while he attended the coronation Shane and I sat home, because I couldn't find a babysitter. If it hadn't been for the piano in the garage, I think I would have gone stir crazy.

Jan Bishop

During school I reluctantly began to get involved in some new types of ministry. The Bible Institute had a program that reached into the local community with a variety of evangelistic opportunities. There was an older lady running the program, who had come to the States from Europe some years earlier to sing with revivalist Billy Sunday's crusade team. She asked if I was going to be a part of the outreach team. I said, "No. I left a good job in Chicago to come here to school, and I work a night job just to maintain. I honestly don't have the time."? She believed anyone who did not serve God was making excuses. The first time I saw her after my car wreck she asked, *"Now what is your excuse?"* I was put in charge of leading teams to a nursing home and a penitentiary. I'm not sure why she chose me, but perhaps she saw something in me I could not see in myself. *It is true that "a man's gift makes room for him."* I boldly led the teams, without having the slightest idea of what I was doing, but boy did we learn! It became exciting to see the effect of God's Word and our testimonies on people's lives. God's Word was also having a profound effect upon our lives. For the first time, we discovered that we best take care of ourselves by putting God's interests first. "But seek first the Kingdom of God and His righteousness, and all these things shall be added to you" (Matt. 6:33, NKJV). This scripture shifted our focus from self-preservation to promoting the Kingdom.

The Buffalo Bible Institute was not yet accredited, and I found I would have to attend an accredited college to be accepted at a reputable seminary. After much thought, counsel and prayer it became obvious that we were going to have to leave Buffalo to continue my education at another school. I sent for 28 different catalogs of colleges and systematically narrowed them down one by one. Finally we came up with a Southern Baptist school called Carson-Newman College in Jefferson City, Tennessee.

We made preparations to move south, feeling that the worst was behind us. We had persevered through suffering, learned from our afflictions and had seen God deliver us again and again. Looking back, we can see that we had barely made a single step along the road to *ground zero.*

We left Buffalo in July of 1963 and finally felt that we were firmly nestled in the hollow of God's hand. our excitement soon turned to disappointment. I enrolled in Carson-Newman College to study the Bible, but found the Bible department to be totally different from the Buffalo Bible Institute. I had been taught at Buffalo that the whole Bible was the inspired Word of God. My Old Testament professor at Carson-Newman did not believe that Moses wrote the first five books of the Bible and did not believe that Isaiah wrote his book. In the course of the Book of Acts the professor taught that all the supernatural works of the early Church were over. It seemed that Carson-Newman College had reduced the Bible to an inaccurate history book. Disillusioned I began to take psychology courses, for in them I saw something that was useful and helpful. I switched my major from Bible to Psychology, hoping to find some answers for my own life.

It was really difficult trying to work my way through school and support my family, so I figured it would be in my best interest to get to know the professors. This did not always bring the results that I had hoped.

Fred had to take a class one semester in Children's Literature. I always thought Fred was a teacher's pet when it came to school. The instructor was an older woman who had a reputation for being very tough and demanding upon her students. Fred didn't consider the class important, so he didn't study much for it. He thought if he could get to know the teacher really well she would let him slide by. From the first day of class, the instructor called Fred the name of another man in the class, named Jim. Fred tried correcting her a few times but finally gave up, and "Jim" soon became her favorite student. She would often call out to Fred on campus, "How are you today, Jim?" and Fred would say, "Just fine, Professor." On the day after final exams Fred saw her walking across the campus and rushed up to see how he did in the class. She got out her grade book and said, "Jim, I'm so proud of the effort you put forth in class this semester. You made a very good grade, I'm glad you're not like that Fred Bishop in the class, who just barely squeaked by!"

Jan Bishop

While in school Jan and I both worked at a snack bar in the student center, called the "Canteen." We lived just off campus in a government housing project with many other students who had families. We became very close with a couple named Gene and Jama Shephard. Jama had a knack for making her apartment look like it came out of a decorating magazine, though they didn't have any more money to spend on decor than anyone else. Jan learned decorating from Jama, and as a result, no matter where we have lived, our homes have been beautifully decorated. No one can turn a house into a home like Jan. Jan's lessons in interior design came to a sudden halt on October 8, 1964, when our daughter Jill Yvonn was born in Morristown, Tennessee. Our family was now complete, and I set my hand to the task of graduating from college.

When I graduated in August of 1966 it was time to choose a seminary. We determined that I would go to Southwestern Baptist Theological Seminary in Fort Worth, Texas. I had heard that the professors there believed the Bible to be true, and I was anxious to get the opportunity to attend! We excitedly moved to Fort Worth, Texas, and enrolled in the seminary. I began to study and learn.

As always I had to work to support my family. My first year I worked full time at a Piggly Wiggly grocery store and carried a full load at school. My second year I took on the added responsibility of the pastorate of the Oakwood Baptist Church in Forth Worth. One of the interview questions their search committee asked me was how I felt about speaking in tongues. I said, "Why pray for a thousand tongues, when you don't use the one you have?" My problem was not a lack of tongues, my problem was figuring out how to properly use the one I had. Soon after accepting the invitation at Oakwood I met a man who would play a major role in my life, Murphree Carlock. Murphree was formerly a bull rider and currently a stock-car driver, who loved to share his faith with others.

> Murphree was the image of a real Texas cowboy. I never saw him when he was not attired in western clothes, cowboy boots, a cowboy hat and a slow Texas drawl. He didn't live on a ranch or own a horse, but at any time I expected him to come riding up on one. On one occasion, while Murphree was witnessing, a man in the bar became angry and hit him in the mouth. Murphree shrugged, picked up his hat off the floor and drawled, "I could hit harder than that when I was a little kid."
>
> Jan Bishop

Oakwood was made up largely of people who had been discontented in other churches, and they naturally brought their problems with them. Jan developed a bleeding ulcer and lost a lot of weight, because of the stress. I thought the answer to all of life's problems was a better education. If I could study a little harder and learn a little more surely I would have something to offer these people.

My inner compulsion kept me going, but my body could not bear the pressure. I was going to school all day, would work from early afternoon until 11 p.m. and go home to study, prepare sermons and sleep before going back to school. I finally went to the doctor one day and said, "I am feeling so weak that I can't even climb the stairs to my second floor apartment." He said, "Kick your feet in the air." I began to get dizzy after the third kick. My cholesterol reading was 289, and he said, "You're stressed out, and you're working too hard." I explained, "I can't back off anything I'm doing right now." He replied, "That's O.K., young corpses look the best." That scared the "puddin'" out of me! The church received my resignation the next week.

Despite my adjusted schedule I still had some uneasiness within me. I was about to graduate from seminary, and I still didn't have the answers to the real-life problems that people face. I had been hoping that the answers to life's problems would be found in the next course or the next degree. The courses were helpful, but they were not the total answer. It was really scary to be reaching the end of my seminary education, having taken all my courses and knowing I had no real answers.

In the fall of 1969 several seminarians received invitations to go to Dallas, Texas, for a conference at the Marriott Inn. The conference centered around the need to have power with God to be effective in ministry. I drove with my best friend, David Church, to Dallas to study under Campus Crusade president, Dr. Bill Bright, and a Presbyterian from Fort Lauderdale, named Dr. James Kennedy. Bill Bright advocated taking door-to-door surveys as a way to win souls for Christ. James Kennedy proposed a set of questions he felt would lead toward conviction and soul-winning. We all learned a great deal from these two men. After the conference I could do more with the *Four Spiritual Laws* curriculum, Campus Crusade's survey sheets and a couple of simple questions than I could do with three years of seminary courses. This was exciting, but there had to be more.

In my last year of seminary a movement of God came to our campus, which my Baptist theology could not explain. For a time, in each chapel service many students would be convicted of their sins in an emotional and powerful way. I remember sitting in chapel and crying. After the formal chapel service was over many would move to a tiny prayer room in the basement, and we would lie on the floor crying. What could this mean for my life? I had already confessed my sins and asked God's forgiveness, but this conviction made me feel so unworthy. I did not get a satisfactory interpretation of what was happening at Southwestern during my last year of seminary, but I was glad to be a part of it.

During his period Jan attended a meeting that offered an explanation for what I was experiencing at chapel. They taught her that being filled with the holy Spirit was an experience that comes after salvation. (When I was a boy in the Methodist church an experience very much like this was called "sanctification.") Jan went forward, and God greeted her with the baptism of the Holy Spirit. She knew I was against this so she didn't tell me what had happened to her. It was ironic that Jan finally had some victory in her life, but I, despite my education, remained frustrated. I heard God's Spirit calling me to deeper things, but could make no sense of it nor find a way to pursue it.

Though frustrating for me the last year of seminary was most enjoyable for Jan and the kids. Shane was in grade school, and Jill could go to the seminary nursery program while Jan took the opportunity to take some seminary classes. The seminary "village" of apartments made for good friendships and eased the pressure financially. For us life was uncommonly tranquil and good.

Just before graduation I was informed by the school that I had missed a necessary core class. The letter said my only options were to stay another semester and take the class or drop out of school without a degree. Exhausted and angry I marched into the dean's office. "I have worked full time for three and a half years to get through school, and I can't take it anymore. My family is leaving Forth Worth in December whether I have a degree or not." God indeed moves the hearts of kings, rulers and deans. In an unprecedented move the administration voted to waive the class requirement for me. I graduated with my class in December of 1969.

It felt good to be out of school, though I was haunted by the lack of an explanation as to what was trying to happen in the chapel services. I found out later that in the spring semester of 1970 some students came to Southwestern from Asbury Seminary in Wilmore, Kentucky. They reported a similar move of God at their school, which had sparked a full-fledged revival. Sometimes I wonder if I should have stayed another semester and experienced the revival.

I graduated from seminary still looking for answers, but there was no time for regrets. There was work to be done! We were building a road to *ground zero*.

Chapter III

Baptized With Struggle

In December of 1969 I graduated from Southwestern Baptist Seminary and promptly accepted the pastorate of Oak Grove Baptist Church, three miles north of Pinckneyville, Illinois. The church had an attendance of about 130 people. We wanted to move back to southern Illinois to be closer to our families, so the Oak Grove invitation seemed like a good one. The church had a lot of very fine people in it, but it was a preacher eater. Oak Grove had gone through 17 pastors in 28 years.

> While we were still living in Forth Worth we had been notified of the opening at Oak Grove by Nine Mile Associational Missionary, John Whitmer. We were put in touch with the church, and they asked Fred to come up to preach and interview with them one Sunday. Fred was the produce manager of a Piggly Wiggly store and

not only had to take off work without pay, he had to hire a man to fill his pulpit out of his own pocket. They sent down a plane ticket, and we scraped together all the money we had in the world to get up to Illinois. Fred went up, preached and interviewed. He was paid $15 to cover his expenses. That should have told us something.

Jan Bishop

Though the church asked me to be the new pastor, the vote was far from unanimous; there were people in the church trying to fire me before I had even arrived! I was determined not to be the 18th pastor to be chased from the pulpit of Oak Grove, but it would not be up to me. Despite my determination to stay I must confess that it was several months before we had the confidence to unpack our boxes and bags.

While still in Ft. Worth I had bought a red Yamaha 250 motorcycle to relieve stress. We brought the bike with us to Pinckneyville, and we rode around in the afternoons attempting to get acquainted with the countryside and reacquainted with each other. After three and a half years of working in a grocery store 40 hours a week, pastoring a small church and attending seminary full time, Jan and I found we had a lot of catching up to do. I also had some catching up to do with the kids. Shane was midway through third grade, and Jill was in first grade. Jan had actually raised the children by herself, and our lives had grown apart due to a lack of time together.

It was immediately obvious that Jan's way of doing things and my way of doing things were totally different. I had answers fresh from seminary classes on everything from child rearing to church growth. Jan did everything by instinct, praying a lot and acting from her heart. It was clear that Jan had a quality that I had never seen in her before, but I did not yet realize she had been filled with the Holy Spirit.

As time passed I began to settle into my work and continued riding the motorcycle. A lot of the young people in the area had cycles, and it gave us something in common to talk about. I started having the teenagers over to the house to look at motorcycle magazines, and our informal get-togethers soon turned into Bible studies. Lots of teens came and were quite open with us. When I started inviting the teenagers to church I was shocked at their honest responses. When I invited one young man he looked at me like I was crazy and said, "Why should we come to your church? Your church leaders can't even give up smoking. How are they going to tell us how to give up drugs?" I felt like I had been kicked by a mule. What a question! The problem was I didn't have a good answer. I told the deacons that if they would just quit smoking we could get a lot of youth into the church. But they couldn't quit.

As I learned to care and to listen to people I began finding out that many had big problems, ranging from crumbling finances to closet homosexuality. *The fact was I did not have an answer for anyone's problems, not even my own.* There I stood, the Rev. Fred L. Bishop, out of college with a psychology degree, out of seminary with a Master of Divinity degree and utterly unable to help anyone. Did God bring me here as some sort of cruel joke?

One day a man asked me to come to his house, because he and his wife needed marriage counseling. On my way out Jan asked where I was going, and I told her. She looked at me with stony eyes and said, "What in the world are you going to tell them?" I told her, "What I learned in counseling classes." She retorted, "If you really knew anything about happy marriages you could practice it right here in our own home!" What a blow! The young people on the streets had hit me hard, but Jan dealt a death blow with her reply. In sheer frustration I went to talk to the couple. They ended up getting a divorce. One year out of seminary, and I was already at rock bottom and out of answers.

About this time, in 1972, my old friend Murphree Carlock started sending me books. I knew he had been filled with the Holy Spirit, and I did not want to read them. But because I was grasping at straws, I reluctantly started reading his materials. To make matters worse, Jan found an old Full Gospel Businessmen's magazine, called *Voice,* at the laundromat in town. I was sitting on the floor of the kitchen when she came home and asked me to read an article that she said fit me to a tee. Despite how poorly life in general was going and despite my frustration, I had to draw a line somewhere. "I'm not going to read that trash." At my refusal she angrily threw the book on the kitchen floor and stormed out of the house.

Perhaps just one article wouldn't hurt. As I read, it seemed like the man in the article was me. His life symbolized all my frustrations. He realized education alone was not the answer to the real-life problems people face. The man became baptized in the Spirit and finally found the power for ministry he had lacked. In front of me was a possible answer to the questions I had been asking for all these years. Not being one to quickly jump to another theological camp, I began studying the baptism of the Holy Spirit.

The books that Murphree Carlock had sent me told of experiences that were absolutely overwhelming, but they would not line up with my theology. I read *The Cross and the Switchblade* by David Wilkerson. The outcome was great, but did that make the methodology acceptable? *A Taste Of New Wine* by Keith Miller was a great help, but the book that helped me the most was *A New Song* by Pat Boone. Boone told how his wife became filled with the Holy Spirit. It spoke to my heart, but my mind was still not convinced.

In the meantime I focused my energies toward the ministry of Oak Grove Baptist Church. Member for member we probably had more programs than any church in America. The church sponsored two softball teams, fast pitch and slow pitch, that involved about 30 guys. I took the church on hikes—hikes for little children, hikes for old people, hikes for other groups. We had every kind of a program you could think of, but Jan refused to go to any of these events, because she knew they weren't working. One day she scolded me, "You have all these events, all these programs, but can you tell me one person, just one, who has been changed by Jesus Christ?" After some thought I came up with one man who played on the ball team. A few weeks after our conversation he not only quit the team, he quit the church and did not come back.

After a rocky first year at the church we needed a breath of fresh air, so we decided to take a vacation to sort it all out. We took Jan's mother to St. Augustine, Florida, with us for a time of relaxation and reevaluation. It was a miserable trip. While body surfing on the ocean I injured by back, and we had to return home early. Upon my return I was put in traction in the hospital. While I was there one of our softball players came in and told me that our third baseman had "cussed out" the umpire during the last game. It was obvious my programs were not producing the life of Jesus Christ. Everything was crumbling before my eyes. There was not a single person who had been changed by all my innovative and progressive ideas.

I needed to talk to someone. There was a friend of mine who was a local pastor, and he had recently preached a revival at our church. I drove down to talk to him and blurted out, "I'm considering getting baptized in the Holy Spirit." He said there was nothing to it, and we ended up telling each other how great we were and bragging about all the things we were doing in our churches. As I was leaving he said, "By the way, Fred, my wife is leaving me." That was the last straw. While driving home on Route 127 something began to move within me, and I began to cry out to God. Some kind of dam was about to burst. I said, "God, I know I'm saved, but I am absolutely powerless and cannot help anyone." Since so many people had said the baptism of the Spirit was demonic, I tried to keep focused by singing songs about Jesus.

I had been spending time for months trying to get my life right before God. I had asked forgiveness for everything imaginable. Jan and I were still having our problems, and I began to think, "What if we got a divorce?" The first thought that came to mind was that I would lose the church. I didn't really care about my wife, I just cared about being a pastor! I could hear God saying, "You don't love Me. You love the church." My biggest fear of getting baptized in the Spirit involved the realization that it would not fit in with the theology of most Baptists, and I could lose the church. God again spoke to me saying, "It's not your church. It's My church. You don't love Me. You love your work, and I'm a jealous God." The impact was revolutionary!

As I fought the tears I began to give the things I held most dearly over to God. I released to God my wife, the kids, the pastorate and finally my life. As this occurred my mind's eye could see Jesus sitting in a big rocking chair, and I ran over and crawled into His lap. "Jesus, I'm not a good father." He replied, "I know." "I'm not a good husband." He said, "I know." I said, "I'm not a good pastor," and He said, "I know." At that moment I realized that though Jesus knew all my failures, He loved me anyway.

I experienced in that envisioned rocking chair the unconditional love of Christ. It was in that moment I prayed and asked God to fill me with the Holy Spirit. Still driving, I felt like there was a big funnel on top of my head, and God's Spirit came down. I was instantly engulfed in waves of "liquid love." God's Spirit ministered healing to me mentally, emotionally, physically and spiritually. I received the baptism by faith, just as I had received salvation at the age of 14. Was this the experience I had been waiting for my whole life?

The books I had read said that when people receive the baptism of Holy Spirit, they often speak in tongues. I didn't know how, so I said, "la, la, la." To an observer, seeing a grown man weeping in a car and saying la, la, la would probably seem absurd. I could not have cared less! I had my mind and my emotions centered on Jesus, and He was flooding me with the Holy Spirit.

The sensation was one of absolute forgiveness and total cleansing. I was so engulfed by God's Spirit it even felt like my fingernails were clean. That may not mean much to most people, but growing up on the farm I never had clean fingernails! I felt squeaky clean from the top of my head to the bottom of my feet for the first time in my life. The answer had arrived! It was not in intellect, not in education, it was in the message of Jesus Christ. He said, "Tarry in Jerusalem until the Holy Ghost comes upon you" (see Luke 24:44). Pentecost had come for me, and my life would never be the same.

When I got home I could not wait to relay to Jan what had happened to me. Excitedly I began spinning the tale and, as I am prone to do, soon got sidetracked by telling long stories and beating around the bush. She finally tired of waiting on me and said, "Fred, did you get baptized in the Holy Spirit or not?" The answer was an emphatic, "*Yes!*"

> For two years I have been praying that Fred would experience the victory in his life that I had since receiving the baptism of the Spirit in Fort Worth. When Fred finally received the Spirit for himself his whole outlook on the ministry changed overnight. He started letting God lead him, rather than hoping God would fit into all his ideas and programs. I think the experience answered a lot of questions he had, and for the first time in his life he was ready for effective ministry.
>
> Jan Bishop

Something had happened to me that summer of 1972, in a life-changing sense. I knew things would never be the same, but didn't yet realize how different the baptism of the Spirit would make me. I began my retooled concept of ministry by leading the church in a study on the gifts of the Spirit. As I shared on the gifts with my new-found fervor, the congregation looked at me as though I were from another planet. Who could have guessed where this new-found walk with God would take me or the trouble it would bring.

My first opportunity for ministry on a large scale came in the late summer when I went to Kankakee to be the keynote speaker for Three Rivers Baptist Association youth camp. I honestly considered canceling, since people were treating me so strangely, but I received the brochure from the camp, which stated the theme, "Be not drunken with wine, but filled with the Holy Spirit." Now this was exciting! These people must be going through the same frustrations I had experienced and now wanted me to lead them into the baptism of the Spirit!

Jan and I drove through a thick fog to get to the train station in Carbondale, Illinois. As we anxiously crept down Rt. 51 it became apparent we were going to miss the train. When we finally arrived I hurriedly bought my ticket and looked up to see the train moving! I slung my bags over a car rail and jumped from the platform, catching the rail with one hand. The conductor saw me hanging there and began yelling, "Man hanging off the train, man hanging off the train!" The trip clearly went downhill from there.

Upon arrival at the Kankakee station no one was there to pick me up, but things soon seemed brighter. After all, I had the power to do ministry, and this was my big opportunity! Finally at the camp I got settled into my cabin and began looking for some folks with which to share the changes that had happened in my life.

On the third day a camp official stood with me in the lunch line. He said, "You have been talking a lot about Pat Boone. Do you know he speaks in tongues?" I casually replied, "Yes." The man looked at me more intently and followed, "Do you speak in tongues?" I replied, "Yes." The man excused himself, and I ate alone. When I returned to my cabin it was crowded with preachers and camp leaders armed for an inquisition. The Associational Missionary repeated the questions the official had asked earlier, and I responded the same. He told me they thought I had experienced a lot of trauma in my life and was way off base with the tongues thing. They said the position was heresy to Southern Baptist doctrine and informed me that I was to leave the camp immediately.

Slowly it sank in—they had just kicked me out. They told the kids that I had to leave for an emergency, and they asked me to stay at a local hotel until I could find a way home. The whole thing was perplexing to me, but I was too high on the Spirit to let it get me down. I called Jan to come and pick me up. She had earlier formed a singing group called "Joy" with some of the teenage girls in the church, and they were on their way to sing in northern Illinois at the church we had attended in Somonauk. "Joy" picked up an unexpected guest, and we all had a great trip.

Upon our return home the camp officials sent me a copy of the letter they were sending to the Illinois Southern Baptist headquarters in Springfield. The leaders flatly said I was a heretic and should not be allowed to minister in the Southern Baptist organization. As I read the letter the seriousness of the whole situation hit for the first time: these people were trying to ruin me! How frustrating it was to finally have something to offer people which could give them victory in their Christian walks and not be allowed to share it with anyone.

Looking back I don't have any hard feelings toward those who wrote the letter. The ministers at Kankakee were just trying to protect their kids from something that scared them. To their credit, in the process they had made a sound suggestion to me. They told me of a young Baptist evangelist in Chicago, name Sammy Tippit, who had been getting a lot of press. They informed me that he was leading a lot more people to Christ than I was, and he wasn't off on this fullness of the Spirit/tongues thing. They suggested I board the next train to Chicago and get myself straightened out.

Jan and I sat down and tried to rationally decide what direction we should go with our lives and ministry. I took a quick career assessment and determined I had been officially ostracized by my denomination and publicly humiliated in front of my peers. We still had Oak Grove, but that, too, could soon be in jeopardy. There was no rational way to approach the situation, so we began to seek God as to the direction of our lives. The only lead I had with which to put my ministry back on track was the name of a guy in Chicago. I could not have dreamed how intertwined the next five years of my life would become with the life of a young evangelist named Sammy Tippit. We had made some significant strides down the road to *ground zero.*

Chapter IV

Nonconventional God

It was 1972, and I found myself in a surprisingly good position for ministry at Oak Grove Baptist Church. Recently filled with the Spirit and ostracized by the Baptist hierarchy I really had nothing to lose by setting out on a radical course of leadership in my church. The focus of my ministry was the young people in Pinckneyville, Illinois, who had "turned on" to God as a result of the Jesus movement that swept the United States in the late 1960's and early 1970's.

Looking back at these years at Oak Grove I see them as the proverbial best of times and worst of times. On the plus side, many people were being saved, delivered and filled with the Spirit. We were doing evangelism in such a way that the community could not ignore what was happening at Oak Grove. To balance the good points, many of the old guard from the church began to feel alienated from what was happening.

> Once I got involved in the Oak Grove Church it became obvious to me that there were some people trying to get Fred out. Every month at the business meeting a motion would be made to remove him from being pastor of the church. All of the youth and young families who had joined attended church every time the doors opened, including business meetings. Our votes kept Fred from getting ousted each month by the church's old guard.
> Fred Starkweather

I had been under fire since I had arrived, but as God continued to move in ways most people didn't understand, my position as pastor became more and more vulnerable.

At the advice of the officials who kicked me out of the Kankakee youth camp I went up to Chicago to meet Sammy Tippit. The first thing that struck me about Sammy was that he looked more like a football player with a boyish face than he did a preacher. It did not take long to discover that he had more vision than anyone I had ever met. Sometimes Sammy would get so caught up in his dreams that he seemed to be off in another world. He had great preaching and teaching skills and used them to make disciples, which was the central focus of his ministry. At the headquarters of Sammy's ministry, God's Love in Action, I met with

Sam and shared all the adversity I had recently experienced in my life. He shook it off by saying casually, "Man, that's just God's spirit moving." I asked him to come down to Pinckneyville and conduct a Baptist Association youth meeting, and to my surprise he agreed. I returned home encouraged and excited about what God had in store for us.

The anticipation of the youth meeting, coupled with the beginning of the Jesus movement at the high school, touched off an evangelistic explosion in the youth of Pinckneyville. We were passing out Christian literature and encouraging the young people to write their book reports on books like *The Cross and The Switchblade*. Art students began to draw pictures laced with Christian symbolism. The much-anticipated Baptist Association youth meeting was held at Pinckneyville First Baptist Church. There were 1,100 young people in attendance. This broke our previous record of 90, which was achieved on a roller skating night. The meeting was powerful, and it resulted in many more decisions for Christ. Revival had come to the youth of Pinckneyville!

To follow up the youth meeting Sammy agreed to come to Oak Grove and preach a revival. He brought his singing group called Living Water. We averaged about 500 people each night in our small country church by seating folks on chairs, the floor and the window sills. I suggested to Sammy that we take Living Water and hold a meeting right next to the high school in Pinckneyville. After we talked to the chief of police it was agreed that the city would block off the street for us across from the school. We set up the sound system on a truck flat-bed and put our Christian rock band out there as soon as school was out. The kids all came over, and many started coming to the revival. I was in the first real church revival of my life, and even though the meetings soon concluded, the revival wasn't nearly over!

During this time our children, Shane and Jill, were attending a country school called Community Consolidated District 212. As the shock waves of revival spread to this grade school some older kids asked me to come and share. They were sent some tracts to pass out, and I planned to personally follow up the next week. When I arrived at the school the kids met me at the door. They said they no longer needed me to come. The kids said, "We have already witnessed to everyone, and they have almost all accepted Christ!" There were very few young people in that little school who didn't give their lives to Christ that year.

The enormous energy of this local revival was soon turned outward, and we began to actively witness in southern Illinois. We witnessed in parks and in small towns, and we even made a huge wooden cross and carried it through Jan's hometown of Tamaroa.

The Oak Grove Church had been growing by leaps and bounds, and the Lord was sending Oak Grove many young families. Two of these families

Nonconventional God

have remained our dear friends and partners in ministry. Gerald and Carolyn Wright and their daughters, Michelle and Kim, started at the church because of Michelle. Gerald was a coal miner who worked seven days a week. One day Michelle asked him why all the other little girls' daddies took them to church and he didn't take her.

> When I decided to get us involved in a church we chose to visit Oak Grove. Oak Grove had a reputation around Pinckneyville as being a church where things were happening. They had a young preacher who rode around on a motorcycle and spent most of his time witnessing. The first Sunday we visited, Fred was in the hospital with a bad case of poison ivy. His family had been out in the country riding motorcycles, and he had to use the restroom in the woods. He apparently sat in the wrong spot. When I did meet Fred it was his enthusiasm and zeal that attracted me to him. Fred was bubbly with the Spirit of God and had a way of talking you into doing things that only God could get you out of.
>
> Gerald Wright

Gerald eventually felt the calling to ministry and preached his first sermon at Oak Grove. After preaching for fewer than five minutes Gerald looked apologetically at the congregation and said, "I'm out of soap." An older lady in the congregation asked him if he was sure he was called to preach. Gerald later went to college and did a course of study at seminary; he has pastored several churches in southern Illinois.

Fred and Nancy Starkweather and their two boys, Jeff and James, were introduced to the church by Fred's brother, Rod.

> Fred and Nancy started coming to Oak Grove in early 1972. Fred ran the Dunn apartment complex in Carbondale, so they lived about 35 miles away. Fred also played the drums for a band that played in bars. One night as we were in a prayer meeting, Nancy was overcome by the power of the Holy Spirit and fell out of her chair, slain in the Spirit. Nancy was very active, but Fred seemed reluctant to get involved. Slowly Fred came around and eventually served as church treasurer. I never really got to know them that well in Pinckneyville, but later they became an important part of our lives.
>
> Jan Bishop

Fred Starkweather eventually went to college and did a course of study at Southwestern Baptist Seminary. Fred and I have since made innumerable trips together, and he is one of my dearest friends. He is currently the pastor of the Christian Life Center Church in Herrin, Illinois.

In the midst of this excitement the course of my life was about to change forever. One night a phone call came from Sammy Tippit. Sammy invited me to go witness with his team at the 1972 Democratic National Convention in Miami, Florida. I told him I would pray about it, which is often the religious way of saying, "Not a chance." Jan and I were in St. Louis the next week, and she told me she believed I should go. I told her I couldn't go, because the trip would cost about $165, and we didn't have the money. She retorted, "If you haven't got the faith for $165, you sure don't have any business going." Angrily I said, "If you believe it so much, why don't you go?" She replied, "If I were a man, I would." At that moment she appeared to be more of a man than I was, but I knew right then I would go on the trip. We began to trust God for the money, and people started sharing with us financially in order that I might go.

It was set: Fred Bishop of Sunfield, Illinois, was going to the Democratic National Convention in Miami, Florida, to share Christ! I was excited to get the opportunity to share with others what Christ had done in my life and to learn from Sammy. The word was that when it came to street evangelism, no one did it better.

Once I had decided to make the trip to Miami I asked Fred Starkweather who by then had developed into a leader of the Oak Grove Church, to come with me. There has never been a better person to have on a trip than Fred. A perfectionist with a seemingly endless list of abilities, it honestly seems that there's nothing in the practical realm he can't do. He works slowly and methodically and is an excellent balance to those of us who tend to outrun ourselves. Fred agreed to go with me, and we were off!

> Fred Bishop has always had an interesting effect upon people who have a desire to serve the Lord. He could always seem to get you to do something you didn't want to, get you to think you were enjoying doing it and have you looking forward to doing the next thing you didn't want to do.
>
> Fred Starkweather

I had never been to Miami. What a beautiful place. Soon after we arrived at the convention center Sammy laid out our strategy for witnessing at the convention. As I quietly listened Sammy's plan sounded as exciting as it seemed overwhelming. We were going to put an eight-foot wooden cross outside each candidate's headquarters and another cross at the convention center. There would be at least two people manning each station so that people coming in and going out would see the crosses. We also would be passing out some gospel tracts addressing the crisis in our nation.

As a part of our preparation for the event we attended a city council meeting to see what kind of reception we could expect from the police. The city was having a lot of difficulties with the radical element at the convention and were discussing ways to deal with it. When I say "radicals" I mean groups that were pushing for radical social or political change of one

Nonconventional God

sort or another. Some of these were "yippies" and the "zippies," the "free-love movement" and groups pushing for drug law reforms. They were all very loud, very forceful and, in the case of the zippies, potentially violent. While we were in the meeting I overheard one of the policemen say to the police chief of Miami, "Some of these radicals are passing out leaflets, what do you want me to do with them?" The police chief said, "Nothing." This struck an idea, so I decided to pass out some gospel tracts right there in the council meeting! As the meeting progressed we walked to the front, gave everyone a stack and requested they pass them back. Everyone there thought this was some vital information being passed out, so they all wanted one. Everything was working!

One of the main players in the council meeting was a gentleman named Dr. Ralph Abernathy. Dr. Abernathy represented the masses of poor people in Flamingo Park, who were demonstrating at the convention. The council was trying to get Dr. Abernathy to contain the poor people in the park and not let them roam all over the city. When he came down from addressing the council he walked past me, and I said, "Good morning, Dr. Abernathy." The moment he replied, "Good morning," I got another idea! It occurred to me that Dr. Abernathy was representing so many people, he couldn't possibly remember all their names. He had to act as if he remembered everyone personally, so he surely would have to act that way toward me. I went to the back, and I got a man who was with our team, by the name of Lloyd Cole. We both looked pretty rough. I said, "Lloyd, how would you like to meet Dr. Abernathy?" I took Lloyd to Dr. Abernathy and said, "Sir, I would like for you to meet Lloyd Cole." Dr. Abernathy responded typically, "Oh yes, Lloyd Cole." Lloyd, not missing a beat, said, "Dr. Abernathy, what this country needs is prayer." Dr. Abernathy responded half-heartedly, "Yes sir, this country needs prayer, alright." Lloyd said, "Let's pray," and started leading in prayer for our country right in the council meeting! Dr. Abernathy didn't know what to do!

Our enthusiasm was soon dampened by the news reports of the extreme violence occurring in Flamingo Park. Soberly we realized that our ministry would be taking place in the midst of that chaos. That evening we met back at the headquarters, and Sammy said, "Brothers, we need to talk. Because of all that has been going on in the park, I think we all need to write our wills before we go out tomorrow." Neither my experience at seminary nor the relative security of the pastorate had prepared me for facing martyrdom. Painstakingly I wrote my will, fully expecting to face death in the coming hours. We spent that night confessing all known and unknown sins. Two young men in our group decided the price was too high and returned home the next morning.

The following day Sammy decided we would carry a large, wooden cross through Flamingo Park in the midst of all the radicals. I couldn't imagine us getting through the mob. As we approached Flamingo Park some of the radicals became enraged and surrounded us. Several of them decided that if we liked the cross so much, they would hang us on it. The radical leaders, like a swarm of bees, began to run toward us, but in the twinkling of an eye a man appeared in our midst, seemingly from nowhere. He was an African-American who looked like he was at least seven feet tall. He asked if we minded if he carried the cross through the crowd. With the radicals all running and screaming at us we didn't care if he ate it. He picked up the cross and placed it on his broad shoulders about the time they arrived. The angry mob was full of threats and accusations. Finally they ordered us to leave their park immediately. The newest and tallest member of our team looked at the crowd and said matter-of-factly, "We ain't going nowhere." His English was poor, but his emphasis was strong. The radicals dropped back when he spoke, as though repulsed by his very words. I had never seen such power demonstrated in the spoken word. When the danger had passed, the man disappeared into the crowd, and we never saw him again. I often wonder if God had sent an angel to protect us, and we had been unaware of his identity.

Euphoric at the realization of the power of God in this situation, I suggested to Sammy that we set up a permanent cross right in the radical park! He said, "That's a good idea, brother. You lead the team." Me and my big mouth! I just wanted to be a part of a team, but in a flash Sammy had given me the job, and Fred Starkweather was appointed as my helper. We were assigned to work the site of an organized radical party, and in the flesh our task seemed overwhelming. We were outnumbered several thousand to two, but we believed our God was big enough to do anything.

While working our station we met a man whom I will never forget. The crowd called him "Holy Hubert." Hubert Lindsey was a professional street preacher from California. Hubert had a constant glow about his ruddy, freckled face and was popular with the radicals because of his humorous approach to sharing the gospel. Hubert was a smallish, red-headed man who looked older than he was due to his years on the streets. He wore a Hell's Angels jacket that was given to him by a member of the motorcycle gang whom he had led to Christ. Hubert was a master of the one-liner. When he had the attention of a crowd he would entertain questions. One young radical said, "Hey, Hubert, what is sin?" He grinned and retorted, "Look in the mirror, you little devil." Another inquired, "God made marijuana, who don't you smoke it?" Hubert replied, "God made poison ivy, who don't you chew it?" He was never without words, and God's presence was upon him mightily.

Hubert Lindsey's ministry was one of disruption; ironically, he was doing to the radicals what they were attempting to do to the convention. At a radical

Nonconventional God

demonstration Hubert would stand at the back, and when the speaker would pause he would heckle. He was so interesting that the next thing you knew, he would take over the rally. This did not go over very well with the leadership of the radical elements. Hubert did this at one rally and got the leaders so frustrated that they physically attacked him and started beating him. He had told us previously, "Never pull anyone off me if I get attacked, because when God strikes them He will get you, too." The next thing I knew, the whole rally went into utter and total confusion. Some wanted to let Hubert go, and others wanted to beat him. So the radical factions ended up fighting each other! Hubert quietly walked out of the melee without anyone noticing.

In the midst of political chaos, demonic activity and mob violence I saw God work in a magnitude I had never experienced or imagined in the Church. God demonstrated to us that when you're in God's will you may find yourself outnumbered, but you will never be "outpowered." It occurred to me at that moment that through God's provision I could go anywhere and do anything by the power of His Spirit.

Chapter V

A Giant Step on the Road

Our triumphant return home from the Democratic convention in 1972 absolutely changed the direction of my life. My concept of God grew so big that I was never again satisfied to be a pastor in the country. There was now a vision in my heart that reached beyond the local church, supported by a proven realization that God could do anything through me. With some experience behind us the group I had taken to the Democratic convention felt ready for a new encounter. We decided to attend the 1972 Republican convention, which also was going to be held in Miami. God had come through for us once and we were counting on the same kind of experience happening again.

I was riding high from our recent encounters and was determined to reach farther and dream bigger than I had ever thought possible. A prayer meeting with a group of young people who all were growing in Christ took root at our house. One by one we would pour out our hearts to the Lord, then the next person would add something to the previous person's prayer. It was like putting a puzzle together. No one knew where the pieces would end up, but prayer in this fashion was exciting, especially with a group which was willing to do anything and go anywhere the completed puzzle indicated. Our group consisted of an odd combination of people, ranging from solid young families to teenagers trying to straighten out their lives.

> I remember one night when I was about ten I was listening in on a prayer meeting at the house. They had a time for sharing testimonies, and a new teenager stood up to share. He said that he wanted to thank God for helping him to quit drugs. He had taken his last drug, and he was completely delivered from his habit. After he had finished everyone began to say, "Amen" and hug him. Dad had a funny look on his face and asked him how long it had been since he had taken drugs. The young man didn't even blink when he casually replied, "Yesterday."
>
> Shane L. Bishop

One evening when we were praying a young man named Bill Povolish stayed long after everyone else went home. He didn't seem to want to talk, so I asked him if he needed a place to stay for awhile. He said he could not take living with his alcoholic father anymore. We picked up a house guest. In those exciting times there was no predicting which way the Spirit would move next.

One night we were praying about the upcoming Republican convention and determined the exact amount it would cost each man to go. One man in the prayer meeting offered to drive us down the Miami. In fact he was on his way down the very next day. As we prayed Bill Povolish said he would like to go to the convention, but did not feel any particular call like the rest of us did. Finally he decided that he had nothing else to do and would go if God provided the money. As we each continued in prayer different individuals went over and gave the amount of money God had laid on each of our hearts to help Bill finance his trip. After awhile Bill excitedly exclaimed that he had the exact amount.

The rest of us could not leave the next day, so Fred Starkweather, a licensed pilot among other things, secured his father-in-law's plane to make the trip. Brother Milton Scott, a pastor from Cahokia, Illinois, had brought a young many, Kenny Lynn, with him to the prayer meeting. Kenny got under conviction about going and decided he should make the trip, but would have to first get it okayed with his parents in Cahokia. It was decided that he could fly down with us later in the plane Fred Starkweather would be piloting.

We ended our prayer meeting by taking Bill Povolish out to the Pinckneyville Lake and baptizing him. Barely dry Bill left, riding down to Miami with a Brother McDonald from Sparta. Interestingly enough, Bill would never return from this trip to live in Illinois again. He became involved in a Christian fellowship in Florida and chose not to return with us. At the convention's conclusion Bill had found his *ground zero.* Today he is married and raising a family in Florida.

I preached at Oak Grove the next Sunday morning, and we headed for "Shumeyer International Airport" to depart for Miami, Florida. We joked that at this tiny airport pilots had to use a cow's tail for a windsock. Loading onto the plane were pilot Fred Starkweather, Gerald Wright, Kenny Lynn and myself. Fred Starkweather had charted the course, as we took off for our second great witnessing adventure.

We got as far as Corinth, Mississippi, our first day. We landed at the airport in Corinth and asked the cab driver to take us to the nearest Baptist church so we could attend Sunday evening services. Upon arrival at the church we were so excited that we went around to each person and told about our mission trip. We finally met the pastor, and he was so impressed with our adventure that he asked us to share in the evening service. We had not had any supper, but the church was having an ice-cream social. A family offered to put us up for the night, which worked out very well and saved us some much-needed money. Before we left, the pastor wanted to give us a love offering to help us

A Giant Step on the Road

on our trip. I did not want to accept it, because we had the exact amount we needed, but the pastor insisted, and we left Corinth full of encouragement and zeal.

While flying on to Miami the next day we flew into a violent storm and were forced to land at Titusville, Florida. As we landed we noticed a young boy sitting alone at the airport. This was viewed as a divine appointment, and we shared Christ with him. By the time we left he had given his life to the Lord. The storm raged on, and we saw God's reason for giving us the love offering. We now had an extra night's lodging to cover and some extra meals. As it turned out the love offering from the previous night was the exact amount it took to cover the meals and the lodging.

We left Titusville the next morning for Miami and enjoyed a smooth flight. We got to Miami and found our way to the home where we were staying. We soon discovered that Bill Povolish had arrived without difficulty and had met another young man, who was in a "coffeehouse" ministry. Coffeehouse ministries were informal places where people could get together and talk. They were very popular in the late sixties and early seventies and reached into the counterculture with the message of Christ. Bill and his new friend hit it off great, and they talked all night long. Bill decided to stay in Florida, and he became a part of the ministry team in the coffeehouse.

As we began to pray about the convention and our role in it we felt an oppression by evil spirits connected to the whole scene. We recognized that we were in spiritual warfare and began binding the evil spirits. This binding and casting out of evil spirits was new to us, and as we continued to pray our host's dog began to bark uncontrollably. Brother McDonald said that back home he had been casting out evil spirits and had commanded them to go into a dog out in the yard. When he did, the dog started yelping just like this dog, and then it ran out in the road and was run over by a car. Figuring the evil spirits were trying to go into the dog we commanded the evil spirits to depart from it in the name of Jesus, and the dog immediately settled down.

This experience set an odd tone to the prayer meeting, and the whole thing began to feel very strange and eerie. Someone shared that anyone whose life was not right with God should get it right immediately, because evil spirits could enter any person who did not have his sins covered by the blood of Jesus. Christianity became very serious that night. The next morning one frightened young man went to the airport and flew back home, because he knew his life was not right. He was not willing to let God put his life in order and was too scared of what would happen in Miami if he didn't. All things considered, he made a good choice.

All started well, but we were disappointed that we had not arrived at the convention before it began. There were two primary differences between this convention and the previous Democratic convention.

A Giant Step on the Road

One was that Sammy Tippit was not present to give organization to the Christians' efforts. The second was that the radicals had stayed in Miami during the month between conventions to organize. Tensions were high in the city, and nerves were raw. Both the radicals and the police were ready and willing to wage war with each other. Arriving late and without a plan we got on our knees across from the convention center and began to pray, asking God for direction. When the prayer meeting finished we crossed the street to witness to a group of radicals, who were demonstrating in front of the convention center by burning the American flags off the poles. These demonstrators were our old acquaintances, the infamous zippies. The zippies were a renegade faction which was outcast from the yippies, who were in the Youth International Party led by Jerry Rubin. While we were witnessing to them the National Guard suddenly closed in on us from all sides, standing shoulder to shoulder with riot clubs. Within 30 minutes we had gone from a group in prayer to a group that was about to be hauled off to jail along with a few hundred radicals.

Murphree Carlock had joined us for the trip, and when he saw the police coming he had alertly managed to get outside the circle in time. The rest of our team was gridlocked in the police dragnet, and we could see a convoy of Ryder trucks being brought over to haul the whole lot of us to jail. Murph was on his knees outside the circle praying and holding the wooden cross. In the midst of the confusion Fred

Starkweather went up to one of the guards who was holding a riot club and held up one of our tracts. Fred rationally explained who we were and what we were doing there. A few minutes later this very guard was taken out of the line and put in charge of the whole operation. The first thing he did was to let our group out of the circle. We all were praising God that we did not have to go to jail with that group of about 300 zippies. They would not have made ideal cell mates.

It seemed inevitable there would be many more confrontations between the protesters and the police. The radicals had decided to stage an ultimate demonstration, using their great masses to form a human roadblock along the streets to the convention center on the day when Richard Nixon was to arrive. When Nixon's motorcade approached the convention center the human roadblock would prevent his arrival from any direction. The demonstrators were attempting to overthrow the convention, then and there, with one unified, decisive move. To combat this demonstration the police began to shoot tear gas indiscriminately to disperse the crowd and would chase them from key areas in low-flying helicopters.

We were witnessing in the middle of this mess and had to run through hotels and buildings to escape the tear gas and police helicopters. The police finally tried to clear the streets by using city buses to block off whole streets, overlapping the buses from one side to the other, and guarding the entrances and exits.

A Giant Step on the Road

> I was a coal miner back then, and Fred talked me into taking half of my annual vacation to go to Miami to witness. Fred was so excited about going that it sort of blinded my better judgment. Almost as soon as we had arrived into the violence and confusion I couldn't believe we were there. When I think back to the Republican convention all I can remember is God's provision. It seemed that every situation we ran into, God delivered us. I would like to think He came through because of us, but often I think it was in spite of us.
>
> Gerald Wright

In the midst of all the chaos God gave us great opportunities to share our faith, and we realized God was big enough to handle any situation.

Upon our return home I realized that my call to ministry could not be fulfilled by pastoring the church at Oak Grove. I was trying to do a good job in the pastorate, but my heart longed to reach to other cities, states and even countries. I could hear God calling me to *launch out into the deep;* but where, to what and how? As has so often happened in the crossroads of my life I received a call from Murphree Carlock. He patiently listened as I poured out the desires of my heart to him. I explained that nothing I put my hand to was satisfying and nothing I attempted in the church was met with success. He replied matter-of-factly, "One of two things is wrong. Either the church is going the wrong direction, or you are in the wrong place." I knew that it wasn't the church. With the addition of a new bus ministry things had never looked better. Due to the increased crowds we were even considering an addition to our building. Murphree concluded, "Then you're the one that has gone wrong. God is getting ready to move you out."

Soon afterward Sammy Tippit sent me a cassette tape on which he informed me that he was moving his ministry from Chicago to San Antonio, Texas. He felt God was saying that my family was to move down with them and be a part of the God's Love in Action team. We began to pray about making the move into evangelism. Sammy advised us to get rid of all our debts, because we would be living "a life of faith," and money might be scarce. We later found out that the phrase, "a life of faith," translated into trying to feed a family with no regular salary. Sammy and his wife, Tex, had lived this way for several years, but it would be new to us. Jan and I began to pray and believed it was God's will for us to join God's Love in Action. I resigned from the church, packed our belongings and said good-bye to our home and our security. Good-bye, Pinckneyville. Hello, San Antonio!

Once settled Sam and I began to meet together regularly for prayer and Bible study. It was there that Sam unveiled the burden God had laid on his heart to share Christ at the World Communist Youth Festival to be held in East Berlin, East Germany. As we began

A Giant Step on the Road

to study and seek God's will for us, God began to work. We met first with other people in our church who were involved in full-time ministry, and then just Sammy and I would pray together. We began to memorize scripture passages and the *Four Spiritual Laws* in German. We also translated several simple choruses into German, such as "He is Lord," "God is So Good" and "Alleluia." During these prayerful days a strategy was developed for how to approach the festival. We saw in Acts, Chapter 13, that Paul and Barnabas were sent out as apostles and John Mark was along as a helper. It seemed that Sammy was to function as Paul did, in leading; that I would go in Barnabas' role, as an encourager, and that Fred Starkweather would be asked to go along. We were very excited to have been given direction and now had a clearly drawn plan of attack.

We called Fred Starkweather and shared the vision with him. We invited him to come along as John Mark had gone with Paul and Barnabas. After praying Fred believed he was to join us. We sent him cassette tapes of the material we were memorizing, so he could work on it while in Illinois.

When the time for the World Communist Youth Festival was at hand I brought my family back to Illinois to stay with the Starkweathers, who had since added their third son, Jeremy. When I met with Fred about the trip he seemed light-hearted beyond all human rationality. Fred was excited and whistling as though he were getting ready to go on a family vacation. Deliberately I laid out for Fred the strategy Sammy and I had developed. "Fred, once we get to the festival crowd we are going to work our way to the middle. Sammy is going to preach and tell the people how to get saved, until the communist soldiers haul him off to prison. When they leave I am going to get up and take up where he left off, and when they haul me off you are going to get up and tell the rest of the story, until they haul you off." Fred's jaw dropped, and he said, "You've got to be kidding." He thought he was going along to carry the bags, but we had never been more serious in our lives. Fred was so shaken that he could not fly the plane. The news of our insane plan had sapped all of the energy out of him. As a result Jim Dunn, Fred's father-in-law, flew us to Nashville, Tennessee. We would meet Sammy there, and he would drive us to New York City. I don't recall hearing Fred whistle the rest of the trip.

Sammy, Fred and I had written out our wills and were again expecting to die as martyrs, as we left for the World Communist Youth Festival. Our trio was convinced we had heard God on the matter, and I don't think any one of us really thought we ever would return. We drove to New York City and upon arriving at the airport began witnessing to people, especially anyone who appeared to be German. We wanted to practice the language. One of us would go up to a German-speaking person and ask if we could have some help with pronunciation of some of the words. The words just happened to be in our *Four Spiritual Laws* booklets. This proved to be a very good method of entering an opportunity to witness. We finally boarded the plane and took off. I noticed the girl sitting next to me was drinking a cocktail and, without so much as introducing myself, blurted out, "What do you think would happen to you if this plane were to crash into the ground or the ocean?" She looked at me with repugnance and said, "I think you're morbid!" She was right! When you're convinced that you are going to face certain death it doesn't make any difference whether they shoot you in East Germany or if you die in a plane crash. You're still dead. I was going to East Germany to die.

As the plane flew across the Atlantic I felt guilty, because I had bought a 30-day life insurance policy before leaving for the trip. It seemed like stealing from the insurance company. As I weighed it out I concluded it was better to take the money from the insurance company than to die and leave my family with nothing. All my experience, training and preparation had come down to this moment in time. Perhaps, "For this day [mission] I was born."

Chapter VI

The Color of Ministry

In the summer of 1973, after months of preparation, Sammy Tippit, Fred Starkweather and I finally arrived in Germany to share Christ at the World Communist Youth Festival in East Berlin. When we arrived in Frankfurt, West Germany, the media came out with a news bulletin that said no Westerners would be allowed across the border to attend the communist festival. We thought, "What are we going to do?" As we prayed we believed God said, "Stand, and I will open a door that no man can close." In faith we packed everything up and headed for East Berlin. We deduced that either we had received some misinformation, or we had missed God for the past several months. When we arrived in West Berlin we put our suitcases in storage at the train station and went to test the "closed" border to East Berlin. When we went cleanly through the border we just wanted to stick out our tongues at the devil and say, "You lied."

The communist festival was not going to start for a few days, so Sammy decided that we could systematically smuggle the Bibles and tracts over to the communist side in advance. We stuffed Bibles and tracts in our clothing and traveled through checkpoints as tourists on a daily visa. Once across we hid the materials, so that when the communist festival started we would have them to use. Smuggling the literature across the border proved easier than finding a place to hide it. We finally hid the literature in a park just outside the Russian military base in East Berlin. Sammy thought that no one would think of looking for it there.

Fred Starkweather has always amazed me with his sense of direction. If he has been somewhere once he can always remember exactly how to get back. The next day we were praying, and Fred believed that God showed that he should be the one to carry the smuggled materials over the border and hide them in the park. On that first day of smuggling, Fred went across the border, Sammy had an appointment with an old friend, and I was supposed to stay back and pray for them. As I prayed the devil had a field day with my mind, as I convinced myself that Fred was going to be killed smuggling in the materials. I blamed myself for his vainly imagined, fantasized death. I thought, "If I hadn't gotten into all this Holy Spirit stuff Freddie would be alive today. What are you going to tell his wife Nancy? What are you going to tell little Jeff, James and Jeremy?" I have never been as excited to

The Color of Ministry

see anyone as I was that evening when Fred trotted up to the door. The devil had lied again.

The next day we all smuggled more material across the border, with Fred leading the way. As we got close to the park the place was alive with Russian soldiers. Fred decided there were too many of them, so he did an about face and walked past us saying, "No way." Sam and I weren't quite that willing to forget it. We remembered he said the spot was close to a certain area, so we walked into that part of the park. We got to the point and decided the materials had to be under one of the plants. Since you can't just go looking under all the bushes with Russian soldiers standing around, we "cleverly" decided to flip a coin into the air and "accidentally" let it fall to the ground. This gave us an alibi so that we might get a good look under the bushes for the Bibles and tracts. After some inspection we gave up, realizing we couldn't find the spot. Later Fred told us that when he had originally hidden the materials on the previous day some small children had watched him. We deduced the kids must have told their parents, and the military must have come by later and confiscated all of our literature. We were upset that we had lost the materials, but thinking back, it could have been much worse: the soldiers could have confiscated us.

Later in the week, as we were in sight of the checkpoint, Fred made a rather unexpected announcement, "God spoke to my heart this morning and said not to smuggle anything." Fred's proclamation irritated me a great deal. There I was, clothes bulging with Bibles and tracts, and my partner had not bothered to tell me that he was not carrying a thing. Still shaken we continued to move toward the border. Once in line the soldiers walked directly to Fred and ordered him out of the line. They took him in the back to a search area and methodically went through everything he had. Had he been carrying even a single tract or Bible Fred would have been arrested on the spot and faced certain imprisonment. Sam and I would have been searched and certainly detained if Fred had been carrying a single tract. Hearing God has its advantages, but obeying God is a lifesaver.

Our preliminary work completed, the crowds began to pour into East Berlin, and the festival officially began. As we viewed the massive crowds we wondered, "There are only three of us. What are we going to do?"

Though we originally had planned to dress like Europeans and mingle with the crowd we soon found that blending in with the crowd would be impossible. The communist youth all were wearing bright-colored scarves, and we didn't have any. How were we going to share Christ? We decided upon a method of going up to a person and asking the time of day. When the person replied we responded, "Oh, thank you. We have come from America." When they found out that we had come from America they became so excited that they would want us to autograph their scarves. When

I was asked to sign an autograph I would write in German, "God loves you and has a wonderful plan for your life," then sign my name. Fred Starkweather would write in German, "Man's sin has separated him from this plan," and then sign his name. Sammy's line was, "Jesus is the only way to bridge the gap between God and man," before signing his name. We had found a new way to get the gospel in front of people, one of which we had never dreamed.

The officials of the event noticed us right away and at first were under the impression that we were of the American Communist Party. Our unique approach to signing autographs quickly dispelled that myth, and the officials soon recognized us as a potential problem.

In addition to scarf witnessing we developed an equally innovative evangelism method. We would get down on our knees and pray in the middle of the park, assuming that as we did people would gather around us. It worked! Our prayer drew a small crowd, and Sammy started preaching to Fred and me the *Four Spiritual Laws* in German. As other people became curious and began to listen he would take a step back and speak a bit louder. Pretty soon he had a good crowd of people listening to the message of Jesus Christ. We kept waiting for the soldiers to drag us to prison, but none arrived. It seemed that we had hit upon a foolproof method and had finally made an impact upon the festival. Perhaps too much of an impact: the communist leaders were aware of us now and plotting to isolate us.

That night the festival organizers brought in some people who were instructed to literally keep us surrounded. No one was asking for autographs this evening, so we decided to preach. Anytime we tried to preach the group would begin singing and drown us out. Ironically our communist babysitters sang in English. I guess they thought it would be more humiliating. They were singing the hymn made popular during the civil rights movement, "We Shall Overcome." I was stricken by the perversion of applying this song of hope and faith to the Soviet communist ideology. As they sang we knew we had an ace in the hole that could potentially turn this situation around. We knew something they didn't about the song they selected—the other verses. To their surprise we joined with them in their singing. Finally, at the end of the chorus, we led out loudly, singing, "We shall be like Him," and they followed us. We then moved on to "We shall wear a crown." How ironic it was that in the middle of a communist youth festival three American Christians could get several hundred communist youth and soldiers to sing a Christian hymn in English! When the event organizers comprehended the situation they were even more angry. We thought, "The communists may yet win the war against us, but tonight they lost the battle." The crowd was out of their control, their plan had backfired and God was glorified in the most unlikely of places.

The next night we went back, fully intending to initiate another sing-a-long. Immediately upon our arrival we were greeted by an even larger group than the

The Color of Ministry

previous night and were again surrounded. When we tried to sing they started chanting, "Freedom, friendship, solidarity; freedom, friendship, solidarity." As they were screaming we felt neutralized for the first time. We couldn't talk. We couldn't sing. We couldn't do anything. It was a night on which God would have to intervene. And intervene He did!

As we stood pinned in by the screaming crowd it began to rain. The shower turned to a downpour, and everybody split up, running for cover. We found our way to a porch overhang, and a girl wearing a little sign approached us from the crowd. The sign looked like a Jesus sticker. It read, "Jesus is a challenge to my life." We were about to meet our first contact in the East German underground Church. It had taken three days to make our first contact with the illusive underground Christians. They had been watching us throughout the festival and had decided to trust us. They had sent the girl to lead us to them.

We all had read about the underground Church of Eastern Europe, but going to one of their meetings was an experience I'll never forget. After attending our first underground meeting I knew we were going to be in for more than we had bargained for. While we had been reading about them they also had been reading about us! News of the Jesus movement in the United States had excited these folks, and they were eager to see the fruit of it (us) in action. They asked if we really were allowed to have Jesus marches in the public streets. When we answered, "Yes," we found that these were not just casual inquiries. They wanted to have a Jesus march through the middle of the communist festival! What was worse, they wanted us to lead it! The three of us talked it over and decided that since we went there to die this seemed as good a way as any. We organized a Jesus march for the underground Church. At the front of our march we positioned a man with a guitar. The three of us followed him, and the believers filed in behind, singing our German Christian songs. Our march of 200 Christians headed boldly right into the middle of the festival area.

We were well known by the event officials at this point, and every time we came to the park they harassed us. On this night, however, there were over 100,000 people in the park. We quickly drew a crowd of officials as we pushed through the middle of the gathering. They could not catch up with us, so they filed in behind the underground believers at the end of the march, waiting for the crowd to thin so they could overtake us. In addition to our 200 Christians, the 800 to 900 communists following our march pushed our number to over 1,000. I would guess that this was the largest Jesus march conducted in East Berlin during the Cold War period! Once again it seemed that everything the communists did to counter us backfired in their faces. The officials never did catch up to us that night.

The Color of Ministry

We later discovered that before the festival a communist magazine called *Füur Dich* (translated "For You,") had warned that Jesus people might be coming from the United States to disrupt the festival. Everyone at the festival assumed that we were the American Christians written about. To the young people our presence was exciting. They wanted to see the bad guys from the States. Bad guys we were, because all the communist propaganda displayed at the event was anti-United States. The Viet Cong soldiers were being celebrated as the heroes of the communist festival, and Americans were the goats. There were photographs everywhere depicting scenes of American-bombed Vietnamese hospitals, schools and villages. Despite this ploy the communist youth saw us as Jesus people, not American capitalists. Try as the leaders would to sway public opinion against us the idealistic youth viewed us in a more romantic light. If we were criminals from the United States we were certainly charismatic ones.

I never have figured out why the festival officials didn't arrest us immediately and be done with us. If I were one of them that is what I would have done. The only explanation I can give is that God protected us from arrest, but not from annoying the officials. Finally the leaders tired of the game of cat and mouse that they had been losing. A communist leader approached us and stated very clearly that if we continued to disrupt we would be arrested. Disappointedly we returned to the underground Christians and told them we couldn't meet anymore. The Christians looked perplexed, and one speaking for the group said, "Are you afraid to die? We are willing to give our lives for Jesus Christ." With that statement the game changed, and our focus returned. We went back into the streets with boldness, and God miraculously overcame everything the communists did to combat our efforts to minister.

The Eastern European Christians had demonstrated to us the key to effective evangelism. They not only were willing to step out for Christ, they were willing to die for their faith. When you reach that point there is no stopping you!

Our work at the communist youth festival had been a great encouragement for revival. The faith and hope brought to the communist youth festival of 1973 by three men who loved God with reckless abandon had sparked a growing Christian movement. There in the midst of the persecution by the post-World War II communist regime in East Germany, Christianity was not only surviving, but thriving. What a mighty God we serve!

When we stepped on the plane to return home we realized that God had given us an extra and unexpected blessing: we all were alive.

Three men. One week. God's power. Persecuted Christians. Revival.

Chapter VII

Living by Faith?

Upon thinking back, my family must look upon our stay in San Antonio as a bad dream. I had left the security of the pastorate for a job with an evangelistic organization that had no payroll. We were in a day-to-day struggle to pay the bills and put enough food on the table for our family to be nourished.

The highlight of this time, for me, was spending time in prayer, fellowship and study with Sammy Tippit. It did not take long to see what was so remarkable about Sammy. He had quit college and did not have the string of degrees that I had considered essential to ministry. He was gifted as a speaker and teacher, but that was not what made him so special. Sammy's strength in ministry was that he had a heart for God. His heart did not display itself by making Sammy always right. It was when Sammy was wrong that it would manifest itself. When confronted with an area in which he was out of line, he would do the quickest about-face you have ever seen and would repent with all that was in him to get right with God again.

Sammy's commitment to God was nothing short of radical. I remember the day he announced that God had laid on his heart to give away his car, furniture and all his other possessions. It was hard for me to imagine that anyone would do such a thing, but I was with him the day that he did just that. I saw Sammy give away all of his belongings, right down to his son Dave's little chair and the recording equipment he used in the ministry. When God laid something on his heart Sammy would obey it to the fullest extent that he understood. I will never forget the day Sammy emerged from his house as bald as a pickle. We had been confronting several cult groups in our street ministry in San Antonio, and when Sammy's white, gleaming head came out of the house he looked just like one of them. He explained that God had shown him that his long hair had caused him to have pride, so he shaved it all off. I had no doubt that Sammy was a man willing to give his hair, his life and everything in it for the Lord.

The first year in San Antonio was not the kind of thing I would have chosen to put my family through, but we learned to trust God. We were renting a house close to Sammy's in an old subdivision and soon got involved in Gateway Baptist Church. In those fragile

Living by Faith?

times we trusted God both to keep us alive and to make us effective in ministry. At one point that year the only food we had in the house was a single bag of potatoes. That morning we received a call from a lady who said in passing, "If I just had a sack of potatoes I think my family could make it." We gave away the sack of potatoes and trusted God still more. My daughter Jill, the ever-cheerful one, amazed us with her great attitude throughout this difficult time. We didn't have enough money for the kids to buy milk at school, so Jan tried to explain it to them. Jill just smiled and said, "That's okay, we'll drink the juice from our soup." At times we would come home on the day the rent was due with no way to pay it, only to find envelopes of money taped to our door. Once it even came with enough extra to give a tithe of it. At times kids from the church would come to us and give their allowance. I was throwing myself and my family into the ministry in which I believed God was calling us to be involved. We clung to the hope that if God was calling, God would also provide.

As if things weren't tight enough already Fred Starkweather called one day and said that God had laid on his heart to move down to San Antonio and to work with us in ministry. He, Nancy and their three boys left a beautiful house in Pinckneyville that Fred had just built and moved in with us. He couldn't have known what he was getting himself into. When we left Illinois we left all we had in terms of security. A regular salary, pension, insurance and all the benefits of the pastorate were now behind us. The four of us were barely scraping by *before* the Starkweathers came. How were we going to feed five more people? They lived with us for six weeks while looking for a place of their own. Just imagine: four adults, four grade-school-age boys, one young girl and a dog sharing one small house, with one bathroom.

> I don't remember much about our stay in San Antonio, because it all is repressed. I was beaten up, chased home and had my bike stolen the first week of school. It went downhill from there. There is only one pleasant memory of that year. Our house had a large room on the side, that had once been a garage. It was late November, and Jill, Jeff, James and I decided that we needed to put up the Christmas tree. Dad and Fred Starkweather thought it was too early since the weather was still hot and Thanksgiving wasn't even here yet. I mobilized our crew into picketers, and we made signs and protested throughout the house. We chanted, "We want the Christmas tree." Dad finally said, "Okay," and we put the tree up that night. There never has been a Christmas tree more beautiful than the one we decorated that evening. It was unlike Dad to give in, but I guess he knew how badly I needed that tree to be up.
> Shane L. Bishop

In the fall of 1973 Fred Starkweather rented the house next-door; now Sammy, Fred and I all lived

Living by Faith?

next-door to each other, with Fred Starkweather's house being in the middle. Life for the Starkweathers was no better alone than it had been with us, and they continued to struggle.

> We all had decided never to mention our financial situations to anyone in our church or elsewhere. Money was so tight that I had to pray before buying a bumper sticker for my van. It said, "I'd rather have Jesus than silver or gold." One night at the end of a scarce month we were out of groceries, and our family had Jell-O for supper. The rent was due the next day, and we had no money to meet the payment. I was doing the Jell-O dishes and literally crying in the dishwater. As I looked out the window I saw that sticker and heard God say, "You bought the sticker; I am going to see if you mean it." We were awakened the next morning by a person who told us that God had shown him that very morning to bring us two sacks of groceries. Two hours later a man came by with a perplexed look on his face. He said that God had shown him to write a check for $135.00 and to give it to me, but he had no idea why. I knew the reason, it was the exact amount needed for the rent.
>
> Fred Starkweather

We believed God had moved us all to San Antonio to do ministry together, and we set about to plan our next venture. Our first notion was to carry a cross from San Antonio to Mexico City. We started studying Spanish, but it just wasn't flying. One day Sammy said, "Brothers, we are going to have to do one of two things: get to taking this Spanish seriously or say, 'Hey, we are not going to Mexico.'" Fred and I believed God was not for us making the outreach. We were so relieved that we celebrated by going downtown and sharing Jesus with people all night. We were relieved there would be no trip to Mexico, but now what?

One of the special things about Gateway Baptist Church in San Antonio was our early morning prayer and share group. Each week we would take turns leading the group and sharing what God was laying on our hearts. One morning a man named Claude Jemmison was leading the group. He was a strange man, who was always telling of the visions and dreams God had given him. He was not a Baptist, and thus some of his visions put our denomination in a bad light. To say the least, what he had to say was not always readily accepted. Despite his eccentricities there was something special about this man. One day I asked him why he came to our denomination, instead of staying in his own where he would be better accepted. He explained that God had spoken to him about wanting to send someone to bring a message to our church. At first he was reluctant to come, but God told him that He could get another prophet if Claude were unwilling to go. God could get another prophet, but Claude could not get another God. One day I pointedly asked

Living by Faith?

him, "Claude, why is it that you have so many words for our church and no words for yourself?" With a sad look he said, "God knows that you are willing to carry out His plans, but I am often not willing to pay the price of seeing them through in my life." I will never forget that response. It became one more milestone in my search for *ground zero*.

One day Claude drew me to his side and said that he had a word for me from God. He said God had shown him why Sammy and I were placed together: Sammy was the one who received the Word, and I was the one with a gift of faith. Claude said these two gifts suited us well for work in Iron Curtain countries. Then Claude said that the same Holy Spirit who gave us power to bind evil spirits in a person would also give us power to bind the evil spirits in a church, a town or even a country. If this were true it could mean there was no limit to what we could do or where we could go for our Lord. Claude then gave me some money he said was to be used for an immediate need. I had many needs, but nothing was pressing at the time.

God spoke to my heart that Sammy and I should go to a quiet place and pray together for the purpose of binding the evil spirits in the towns and countries we were planning to visit. We went to a La Quinta motel and prayed together for some time, until we could tell in our spirits that we had gained the victory over the spirit of fear. Fear seemed to be the controlling spirit behind communism. In fact fear would be so soundly defeated that the day soon would come that we would cross the border into East Berlin just to eat lunch. We knew we had defeated the spirit of communism, at least in relation to our freedom to share the gospel.

As we were praying one night God brought to our memory one of the underground Christian meetings to which we had been invited in East Berlin during the Communist Youth Festival. A young Catholic priest from Bratislava, Czechoslovakia, had asked us to come to his country. He had told us that God had spoken to his heart in prayer and said, "If you will go to the World Communist Youth Festival in East Berlin you will meet Jesus people from the United States." While praying, we could see that young priest pleading with us to come to his country. The apostle Paul, when he received the Macedonian call, could not have seen that person saying, "Come help us," any more clearly than we saw our friend in prayer that day in 1974. There was no doubt we were going to Czechoslovakia! We decided Fred Starkweather should stay in the States and maintain our three families, and Sammy and I would make the trip. The road to *ground zero* would soon get very bumpy, indeed!

Chapter VIII

Singing in the Attic

Sammy and I eagerly made preparations for our initial trip to Czechoslovakia. During our preparations everything fell into place; well, almost everything. Sammy had a head cold that he could not shake. I mean a monster head cold. He was always blowing his nose, and when he talked he sounded like a disc jockey for a bad FM radio station. After some prayer we determined not to let circumstances change our plans. We concluded that Sammy would be healed on the trip. We never could have realized that Sammy's cold would unexpectedly become a catalyst for one of the most spectacular miracles we would ever witness!

Before moving to Chicago Sammy had a ministry in Europe. When he came back stateside he gave the ministry van to his co-workers in Germany. He had made arrangements to have his friends pick us up in Frankfurt in the van, believing they would pray for his healing as well. In faith we boarded the plane and flew to Frankfurt, looking forward to getting Sammy healed. Upon our arrival at the airport Sammy's friends didn't show. I thought to myself, "If this is how our friends treat us...".

Once again our plans blew up in our faces. So we headed for Berlin, head cold and all. As we were riding the train through West Germany we had all the materials we were smuggling hidden inside of our clothes. In West Berlin we successfully smuggled our gospel tracts and Bibles across the border into East Berlin.

We pushed on to Dresden, East Germany, where we met with a group of underground believers in an old, war-torn castle. Despite his head cold Sammy spoke on the Lordship of Christ. At the end of the meeting one young man stood to his feet and said, "Who says we cannot witness for Jesus Christ?" We all knew that the communists were the ones who said we could not witness. Then, without providing the obvious answer to his rhetorical question, he uttered this chilling statement of commitment, "I am willing to die." The meeting ended immediately, with not so much as a benediction.

The following night was one to remember, as each individual had soberly considered the previous night's message and the young man's words. Like dominoes each person stood to his feet and boldly declared, "I am willing to die." I realized this was the real-life manifestation of the scripture that says, "He who has found his life shall lose it, and he who has lost his life for My sake shall find it" (Matt. 10:39, NASV).

One of the believers had tape-recorded some of the events at the communist festival the year before. He let us listen to the tape, and we realized how loud and strong the opposition had been when we shared Christ. Because we had been willing to come to the festival and share Christ openly, we discovered that a mighty move of God had been birthed. In the wake of the festival a few brothers had decided to begin meeting together for prayer. They called their prayer meeting a *Bruderschaft*. Soon they believed they should reach out, and they started inviting others to meet with them. By the end of the summer over 1,500 believers were meeting openly in the city of Grosshartmansdorf.

We were excited and riding high, honestly amazed at the effect of our ministry during the Communist Youth Festival last year still was having in the lives of these people. Eager and encouraged, it was time to move on. We left East Germany to cross into Czechoslovakia. When we arrived at the border the guards routinely came aboard the train to check passports. A young lady was in charge of questioning each person crossing the border. She turned to me and asked, "What is in your pockets?" When she asked I instantly broke into a cold sweat, realizing that I had forgotten to take my Bible out of my back pocket. I had heard story after story of people going to prison for carrying a single Bible. I could hear the prison doors clanging in my ears, and I literally locked up.

Throughout our entire trip Sammy had fought his head cold with a single brave handkerchief. There had not been any place behind the Iron Curtain to wash our clothes, so that handkerchief was green, filthy, damp and full. In my state of panic I instinctively turned away from her, only to see Sammy grinning. Before I could regroup myself enough to answer her question Sammy reached into his back pocket, caught the handkerchief by the corner and mischievously slid it out. When she saw the hankie she shrieked, turned pale and immediately left the train. Needless to say she did not ask to see in one more pocket. Suddenly I realized that we had just experienced a miracle! God was teaching us a very important principle: *when we're moving in God's plan He will provide signs and wonders to confirm His Word.* Signs and wonders aren't to be depended upon for everyday living, but when you're way over your head in Christ's service God will provide in supernatural ways. This instance wouldn't be our last taste of God's supernatural provision.

As we rode the train into Czechoslovakia we rejoiced in the might of our God. Our train arrived in Bratislava, the second largest city in Czechoslovakia, in the middle of the night. We had naively assumed we could make the trip even though we knew only five words in the language. We knew the word "Hallelujah," which is the same in every language, and we knew how to say "Jesus loves you" in the singular and plural. As the train pulled away we realized that the town was not even in sight from the train station. We were tired, hungry, bewildered and most probably lost. We remembered what Art Stacer, a prophet from San Antonio, had said when he prophesied over us at the church before our departure: "The language barrier will be broken in Czechoslovakia." If we ever needed a miracle we needed one now. We walked outside the train station and saw a girl standing by the curb. Sammy asked her if she spoke English. She said, "Yes, what do you need?" God had come through again! She gave us directions, and we finally got checked into a hotel.

The next day we looked around town and went to the university. The gospel tracts we carried were again *The Four Spiritual Laws*. They were written in German, with a German address for follow-up. After some wandering we finally arrived at the place where the priest had asked us to come during last year's World Communist Youth Festival. As we were walking up to the church he saw us coming in the distance. He became so excited that he ran back into the church to thank God for hearing and answering his prayers before even greeting us.

Our game plan was to begin our witnessing outreach at the administrative building of the university. We began phase one by putting tracts all around and letting people come up and get them. The students knew this kind of distribution was illegal, so they quickly snatched up the tracts and put them into their pockets. Still believing the language barrier would be broken I called to two young women coming down the stairs, "Do you speak English?" They informed me they were majoring in English at the university. God had done it again; we knew we were in the right place at the right time!

Time for phase two. We got down on our knees in the center of the building under the rotunda and began praying. We could hear the people gathering around us, and when we had a crowd we began to sing, "Hallelujah, hallelujah." It was our only option since we knew so little of the language. God's Spirit came down on our singing, and a large crowd formed, anxiously waiting for us to say our piece. They wanted to know where we had come from and what we were doing. Many of them understood German or English so we began sharing freely about Jesus Christ. The prophecy had been fulfilled: the language barrier was broken! Our euphoria was interrupted about 45 minutes later when we saw a young man storm out of the room. We sensed we were about to be in big trouble. After all, you can't just go and have a prayer meeting in a communist university, or could you?

The man who had left the administrative hall soon returned with some university officials who attempted to publicly interrogate us. They quickly learned that we didn't speak Czech so they spoke to us in broken German. Their German wasn't very good, so instead of asking, "Where have you come from?" they said, "Where are you?" Sammy's German was very sharp, and he said, "We're right here!" The students who understood what had happened all laughed, but an official calmly restated the question properly. We said, "We're from America." He wanted to know which America. Were we from Canada, Mexico or the United States? So Sammy told him we were from the United States. It was obvious the official had never faced a situation like ours, and he honestly didn't know what to do with us. He had us escorted out of the university complex and told us not to come back.

Perplexed by this turn of events we went back to the church to meet with the priest, and we told him what had happened. When we related our tale he was literally dumbfounded that we had done something so stupid. He told us the police would be looking for us and advised us against going back to our hotel. We had anticipated such an event, and all our luggage had been stored previously at a hotel in which we weren't staying. He took us to retrieve our luggage and on to a private home for safekeeping.

When we went inside we found it was a home where some nuns were living. They were called "illegal nuns." That means they weren't recognized as nuns by the communist government, but they still were ministering. They invited us in and welcomed us with open arms. I saw in them a love for Jesus Christ, evidenced by their willingness to take us in at the risk of their own lives. I realized these were my sisters in Christ Jesus and decided right then, Baptist or not, I was going to change my vote and let at least two nuns into Heaven.

They promptly hid us in the attic of the house, and in the eerie darkness we made out the silhouette of a young priest, who had been in hiding for some time. We introduced ourselves, and I shared with him what we had been doing. In passing I mentioned a worship song we had learned in Germany. The priest asked me to teach it to him, but I couldn't remember all the words. I tried to show him the lyrics written down on a piece of paper I pulled from my pocket, but it was too dark to read. "No problem," he said as he took one of the roof shingles and carefully slid it back. A single ray of sunlight shone down on my crude lyric sheet, and in the attic of an illegal nunnery two Americans and a Czech priest sat in hiding, singing praises to God in German.

We realized that we couldn't stay in hiding forever, so we decided to attempt leaving. As we were attempting to leave we saw a car with two policemen in it sitting right outside the gate. We decided to try walking past them one at a time as casually as possible. Sammy volunteered to go first, figuring if they took off after him he would run, and I would try to make a getaway in the other direction. (It seemed like a good plan to me.) As Sammy walked past the police car the policemen didn't stir, so I started walking. My heart felt like it was going to beat out of my chest as I tried to remember how to look natural. With chest pounding I walked right past them. We had made it out!

Out next task was to find a hotel to stay in for the night. There was a convention being held in town, so all the hotels were booked. This situation provided a positive diversion in that we had to get our minds off our police problem and get back into the day-to-day world. We finally found a "boatel" to stay on. A boatel is a hotel on the water, similar to a large houseboat. It was no coincidence that this boatel had vacancies. As you can imagine, the boat was rocking and reeling all night long, and the beds were just bunks which folded up against the wall. The next morning we took a vote and unanimously decided to find a new place to stay the next night. Unfortunately there was no other lodging available, so we were back to the boatel.

Arrangements had been made previously for us to attend an underground meeting. our contacts arrived at the meeting place and asked us to follow them, but we had to walk half a block behind the others so as not to raise the police's suspicion of the local believers. At that time it could mean a prison sentence for just associating with any Westerner, especially a Christian. The priest who led the underground meeting cut through the formalities and flatly asked, "What are you doing here?" After we told him of our work he wanted to know if we were married. When we told him yes he asked, "What will your wives do while you are in prison?" He related to us how he had been in prison 11 years for his faith in Jesus. We were jolted by the tenor of this conversation. Later we asked various people in the prayer group what differences they had noticed about the priest due to his years in prison. They said the priest had forgotten a lot of the liturgy, but he had a great love for Jesus. We realized that we all might come out better if we were called upon to experience prison for our Lord. Despite this unique growth opportunity we were hoping to pass on it, if at all possible.

One cultural problem in working with the believers in Eastern Europe was they all drank alcoholic beverages. I was determined that I would not drink. At the conclusion of a Catholic prayer meeting the time came for refreshments. Our hosts graciously offered some ale and food to us in the spirit of hospitality. This left me in quite a predicament. Should I offend my hosts or break with my conscience? I suddenly remembered that at another meeting we attended they offered a priest a beer, and he said that he could not drink it, because he was under a vow. Was this my way out of this potentially volatile situation? When it came my turn I answered, "No, I am under a vow from God." The people seemed insulted and bewildered by this, but the priest jumped into action and gave a lesson on vows before the Lord. What a relief!

That night a room opened at a nonfloating hotel, and we finally got a good night's sleep. When we

Singing in the Attic

awakened the next morning Sam said he'd had a dream, which was troubling him. He could hear a voice saying, "Run, baby, run." Things got scary quickly. It was natural to be frightened, and we easily could have run, but we had promised the two English majors at the university we would return and meet with them. I thought it was just our nerves playing tricks on us. On the way back to the university to meet our new contacts we took the addresses of local believers, which we had gathered on the trip thus far, and hid them under a rock in a vacant lot. We did this because a medical doctor we had met told us of the 14 years he had spent in prison for his faith in Jesus. He also told a story of a man who was trying to escape from the Iron Curtain. On the man's way of escape he had stayed overnight with a friend. Later the escapee was caught and arrested. The police found the address of the place where he had spent the night and put those people in jail also. The doctor told us he was willing to go back to prison for the Lord, but not for our stupidity. The story made us all the more mindful of the sacred trust entered into with our oppressed brothers and sisters.

When we arrived at the university only one of the girls came to meet us, and she was visibly shaken. The other girls had been threatened by the police and didn't even show up. "Run, baby, run!" We immediately went to the train station and found that the only train leaving that day for Vienna, Austria, was pulling out in about half an hour. It seemed impossible to take a bus back to the hotel, pack and get back in time, but it appeared to be our only chance to get out. We rushed back to the hotel, where the elevator operator took us up to the 17th floor, locked the door open and helped us pack. We caught another bus back to the train station, and Sammy ran to get the tickets while I carried both suitcases to the train. Sammy joined me on the train just as it was pulling out. We were in the center of God's will, but the pocket sure was narrow.

There was an instantaneous feeling of relief when the train began to leave the station. Our euphoria soon was shattered as the brakes squealed, and the train slid to a grinding halt. We both were afraid that this unscheduled stop was for our benefit. Anxiously we peered out the window and discovered the purpose of the stop. Soldiers were physically removing a group of Jewish people from the train. It was an odd feeling watching racial hatred unfold before my eyes. I must confess to both feeling sorry for them and feeling relieved that I wasn't among them.

It was a great relief finally to reach Vienna and the western world. Upon regaining our faculties we realized it was Thanksgiving day. This realization was so exciting I instantly swung from the pits of despair to the heights of ecstatic fantasy, envisioning myself eating a turkey-and-dressing dinner with my family at home.

Sammy and I proceeded to the airport, fully intending to catch the next flight for home. However, when the ticket-taker looked at our 21-day excursion fare he said, "That will be $100 per person more, please, because you have not stayed the full 21 days." Our hearts sank. Unable to return we decided to send a telegram to let our wives know we were okay. The telegram needed to have as few words as possible to conserve our dwindling financial resources. Mine was to read, "In Czechoslovakia/had to flee/safe in Vienna." However, in the moment of frenzy I forgot to insert the word "safe." What a bummer! My family was significantly more disturbed than if I had never sent a telegram at all.

Checking our resources we found ourselves short of the funds needed to get back to Germany to board the plane on which we were scheduled to leave. We sadly concluded we might have to hitchhike across the Alps—back to the pits of gloom. Enough money was pooled to take a train to Salzburg, Austria. There we stayed at a very inexpensive youth hostel and waited out the remainder of our trip. Most of our time was spent recuperating on a mountain near the hostel. The countryside was a part of the scenery from the movie *The Sound of Music,* and it was absolutely beautiful. Our plan was to spend a couple of days relaxing and trying to get our nerves to quiet down after our ordeal. Our 21 days soon would be over, and we could go home again.

While on the mountain I had a life-changing experience. The Lord spoke to my heart, saying that

Sammy and I had been faithful in doing whatever God wanted us to do, and God was pleased. However, I had ventured so far from "normal life," I was no longer able to challenge other people to serve our Lord. Other Christians listened to my stories and looked at me like I was an alien from another planet. The scripture came to mind which says, "a grain of wheat must fall into the ground and die, or else it will not multiply" (see John 12:24).

My adventurous life was to be transformed by the Spirit into a lifestyle of pouring myself into others that *they* might be used of God. God no longer was interested in using me to make "additions" to His Kingdom, but now would enable me to "multiply" the ministry of Jesus in the lives of many people and in many countries. I now sensed that I had *ground zero* in sight, but my training was not yet complete. I still had a few giant steps to take down the road before being released into my own life's work and ultimate place of ministry.

Chapter IX

So Proud of God

Our first trip to Czechoslovakia opened up new possibilities within the country and penetrated our hearts deeply. Even though we had left the Iron Curtain, the Iron Curtain had certainly not left us. Sammy and I returned to Czechoslovakia the following year, bringing along my old friends Fred Starkweather and Gerald Wright. On the first trip we had seen the need for Bibles and Christian materials in Czechoslovakia and East Germany, so we decided to embark on a large-scale smuggling operation on this trip.

During the past year stateside, Sam and I had shared with everyone we knew about the need to support the suffering Church behind the Iron Curtain. Our zeal greatly exceeded our knowledge in international matters, as some groups and individuals offering to help us were less than honest. One such offer was set up by our friend Ed Human in San Antonio, Texas. Ed said he knew a reporter from *Grit Magazine*. We met with her and excitedly told her of all the encounters we had been through. Later we found that she was an impostor and had no connections with any magazine. She also had a police record as long as your arm and had been accused of extortion by the Mexican government. In another instance we met an underground Christian group which had a newsletter that supposedly raised money to provide Christian materials for people in communist countries. I met with their president and even went on several speaking engagements with him. When I had met with him the first time he was accompanied by the impostor reporter from *Grit Magazine*. I should have been more discerning. We wanted so desperately to help our Christian brothers and sisters behind the Iron Curtain that we were pretty naive about the company we were keeping.

We left for the Eastern Bloc with the sole intention of smuggling materials behind the border and dropping them off with prearranged contacts from the underground Church. To aid in the task Sam had purchased a bright-orange Volkswagen van and customized it for smuggling. Every empty space on the van was arranged to conceal large amounts of materials. When we got to West Berlin, West Germany, we went to the drop point where a Christian group from the States was to have left the materials for our well-orchestrated operation. We were to have 100,000 *Four Spiritual Laws* tracts from Campus Crusade, Bibles and about 800 Christian books. We got to the pickup point and found that an American had been there, but had left nothing. Our spirits sank.

I felt a pang of remorse that I had not come on this trip better prepared. I was especially sorry that I had not bothered to learn more German. Our whole mission was built on the premise that Christian materials not only were needed but necessary enough to warrant the trip. We finally made contact with another group in West Berlin and purchased Christian materials for our mission.

As our quartet neared the border for the first time in our loaded van all four of us realized the gravity of the situation. In one year's time we had moved from being small-time smugglers, who tucked tracts down their pants, to trying to get a fully loaded, customized van through the border. If we were caught we would surely spend years in prison. As we drove up to the checkpoint our minds played tricks on us. I could look in the rearview mirror and literally see the screws twisting out of the top panels of the van, with our tracts forming a trail out the back of the vehicle. Because it was a Volkswagen van, a German product, I was sure that the guards would notice the bulges in the interior panels and order an inspection. We sat waiting in a long line of cars as the border patrol inspected every vehicle. With each passing moment our nerves moved closer to the edge.

We had never crossed a communist border in anything other than a train, and we watched in horror as the soldiers searched every square inch of the cars ahead of us. Seats were taken out of cars, panels were taken off trucks, and an elaborate mirror system checked the underside of all vehicles. They were spending a lot of time at each stop, and as we inched closer my old nemesis, fear, sprang up within my heart. We thought about retreating, but cars had lined up behind us, and we were locked into the traffic grid. There was nowhere to go but forward, and it appeared we didn't stand a chance of making it through the border undetected. Perhaps, after all our adventures in faith our time to go down had arrived.

My imagination ran away with me, as in my mind's eye I could see the soldiers checking the panels and all the Bibles hurtling to the ground. As I inspected our loaded panels they appeared to be so full they were sagging. When we arrived at the checkpoint a woman in charge of the inspection team came out to look over the van. She was well dressed, looked very neat and had obviously just been to the beauty shop to have her hair done. As she stepped out of the office toward us the sky opened up, and rain began to pour from nowhere. The officer grabbed her carefully coiffed hair, looked disgustedly at the cloudburst and snapped, "Oh, go on!" We were the only vehicle in the line they didn't check. God had delivered us again! We were so proud of God.

We headed for Leipzig, East Germany, where our prearranged contacts failed to materialize. Regrouping, we decided to split up. Sam and I went to a disco and began to share tracts and witness like we did so often in the States. It was our unspoken policy that when all else failed we would go back to regular street witnessing. Fred Starkweather and Gerald went in another direction to a bookstore and met a Christian there. He turned out to be a solid contact, and we went to his house to meet with his family. We discovered that East German children had to decide by the eighth grade whether to embrace communism or the Church. If a young person embraced the Church he could not go on to school, so his chances of getting ahead in life were severely limited. Surely God would not allow this atheistic system of government to stand forever!

We went on to Dresden and met with some believers we had known before. They told us of their growth in faith and numbers from the previous year. The Christian meetings, which had grown to number 1,500 as of the year before, now had ballooned to 5,000 and had exploded into five different cities. We rejoiced with them and were awed by what God had done through our World Communist Youth Festival mission. We decided to leave East Germany in the middle of the night, but made a wrong turn and drove up to the border in the wrong place. We were met by startled border guards, barking dogs and spotlights. What a mistake! We finally got to the right road and back into the friendly confines of West Berlin safely.

After a night's rest we went down to the Czechoslovakian Embassy to get a visa for Gerald, since he was a late addition to our group. Fred Starkweather,

Sammy and I had already received our visas before the trip began. We were told that Gerald's would take weeks, but the Lord intervened, and we got his visa within the hour. Our van rolled through West Germany and on to Vienna, Austria, where we were going to enter Czechoslovakia. As we prepared to cross the border Sammy discovered he had left the title papers for the orange VW van in West Berlin. What were we to do now?

Gerald, Fred Starkweather and I decided to go on by train into Czechoslovakia, and Sam would meet us later in West Berlin. We arrived at the train station with our materials hidden in our bags. We decided to search out an empty compartment on the train and transfer the materials from the bags into our clothes, until we could find a more convenient place to hide them. Unfortunately an empty compartment was not to be found, and we had only ten minutes before the train was to leave. We prayed and asked God for direction. The Russian materials were left behind, and only the Czech materials were taken with us. We made it through the border without incident. Things were looking up.

Once in Bratislava, our hotel arrangements soon were made. We went to the seminary to find our Catholic priest contact from the previous trip. To our dismay, the communists had come to the seminary and forced half of the students into the military. Our key contact was one of the students who had been drafted. Now what were we to do? I had a home address for the priest, so we went to his house and met his brother, who also could speak English. I met their parents and began to tell them what an important job their son had done in translating our materials into their language, naively thinking they must be very proud of him. I could not get over the fact that the parents showed no enthusiasm about the stories I told of their son's accomplishments in the underground Church. After we left the house I asked the brother why his parents did not seem excited about the stories I had just conveyed. He told me that he had to change all my stories as his parents did not know their son was connected with the underground Church. Thank God for a sensitive interpreter!

Bratislava behind us, we boarded the train to Prague. Sam was to meet us there if he could get a travel visa. Predictably Sam could not get into the country, and we had to modify our plans. The first item on the agenda was to distribute some of our smuggled materials. Gerald and I entered a bookstore, with one of us on each outside aisle. When the clerk looked toward one of us the other would stuff a tract in each of the books. We honestly had a good time.

Fred Bishop, Fred Starkweather and I had gone into Prague, Czechoslovakia, to smuggle materials, but had missed our contact. It was getting time to catch our train, so we decided to go into a retail bookstore near the station and stock their shelves with Christian literature. We later returned to the store and found our unwelcome addition had been discovered. By the time we reached the train station the streets were crawling with police. We boarded the train and pulled out of the station with the police still scouring the area for us.

Gerald Wright

While the police searched for us we scrambled about, split up, and each one rode different buses on city tours. We gave out tracts and left them everywhere we went, though we made it a point not to leave any tracts in the place from where we were to leave the country.

When it was time for us to meet at the train station we still had a lot of tracts left. We decided to go into the nearby areas and leave tracts in places where people were standing to catch buses. This worked out well, and we were relieved to have our work finished without leaving any evidence which could implicate us.

We proceeded to the railroad station to get our tickets for our trip back to West Berlin. When the ticket-taker saw our passports were from the U.S.A. she began crying. She shared with us that her son was married in another country, and the communists would not even let her go to the wedding. Our hearts went out to her, but we had no way of sharing with her, as we had little knowledge of her language. We already had given away every last piece of literature, so there wasn't even anything we could leave with her. It was concluded there was nothing to be done, since our train was getting ready to leave. Suddenly an announcement came over the loudspeaker, indicating our train's departure time had been delayed. God had intervened on this woman's behalf, and we returned into the night to retrieve some of the tracts that had been dropped at the nearby bus stop. The night had eyes. I saw one man spying on us behind a window. Soon a car came zooming around a corner with its lights beaming directly on us. We thought they were spotlights directed at us; we froze and waited for it to pass. After recovering some tracts and giving them to the woman our trio boarded the train, thinking all our problems were behind us. For the first time on the trip we would be completely legal. None of us were carrying Christian materials. We were just tourists on our way out of the country, right? Wrong!!

When we got to the border between Czechoslovakia and East Germany the border guards routinely checked our visas. Since Gerald had acquired his visa later than we it stated he came into the country in a new van. This mistake had not been detected upon his arrival; therefore, the officials naturally deduced that Gerald had smuggled the van into their country and left it there. The entire train was ordered stopped, and Gerald forcibly was removed from the train for further interrogation.

> The soldiers took me off the train and sat me in a small, dark room. A bright light was shone in my eyes, and an army captain came in to interrogate me. He fired question after question at me about my visa and the van. I told the truth and answered each question honestly. Of all the things they could have arrested us for, I was innocent of this one. The longer he questioned me, the madder the captain got. I don't know if he thought I was lying or if he had been hoping to get a promotion out of catching a black market runner. Finally he marked across my passport and told me never to come back to Czechoslovakia again. I thought, "If you let me out of here, I guarantee you I won't be back." The soldiers escorted me out again, and to my surprise the train was still waiting.
>
> Gerald Wright

One of the problems with traveling together is that each individual's problem becomes everyone's concern. Before Gerald's interrogation we were treated as tourists and given the V.I.P. treatment; the communists liked "rich" Westerners pumping money into their scant economy. Now that we were suspects the tone changed considerably, and the guards decided to reinspect us. To compound the situation I was sick with the flu. As the guards came back and searched through all of our things I remembered about having a booklet in my billfold with the addresses of all the believers we knew. It was too late to hide it. When the guard demanded my wallet my heart sank. Would my carelessness endanger the well-being of the believers we had met? I watched in horror as the soldier gazed at each part of my billfold. He checked everything on both sides of the booklet; it was as if he could not see the booklet jutting out of the wallet. God *can* make seeing eyes blind. We had made it through. We were headed home.

The three of us returned to West Berlin and met Sammy. We boarded the plane thanking God for His protection and guidance on another mission for Him. As I flew home I sensed a chapter in my life was drawing to an end. My apprenticeship to Sammy was over. God had given me a vision for ministry on that mountain in Salzburg, and I now was released to pursue it. God had called me to a ministry of equipping the saints for the work of the ministry. I now would spend my life helping others find their own place in God's Kingdom. My *ground zero* had finally arrived. Getting to *ground zero* was not an arrival at an ultimate destination or the achievement of a sacred goal. It was about finding a beginning. I had reached my *ground zero* without a master plan for ministry, a base of financial support or even a clear place to begin. After all my training, I instinctively knew it was time to stand on my own two feet. I had heard God's call, I had paid my dues, and my moment of truth had arrived.

Finally relaxing during the long flight home I reflected on the images of valuable lessons learned along the path to *ground zero:*

Formal education is of great value. I learned at Buffalo Bible Institute, Carson-Newman College and Southwestern seminary that experience needs a theoretical framework to have its greatest effect in life.

I had seen the principle of being an apprentice, a journeyman and then a craftsman proven to be of great worth. I had served a successful apprenticeship at Oak Grove, and during the 1972 political conventions I had served as a journeyman with God's Love in Action, and now I was ready to begin my ministry as a craftsman with my own organization, No Greater Love.

I saw in myself and in co-workers the truth that "a man's gift makes room for him." God had placed me in positions that maximized my gifts and abilities and had done likewise with friends like Fred Starkweather and Gerald Wright.

We saw God honor our loyalty to His calling for us. Our following His call to Eastern Europe and even making a return trip wrought valuable experience that could not have been attained otherwise.

I saw the Lord honor our obedience time and again. As we would pray and then act accordingly we were spared what seemed unavoidable problems and even imprisonment.

We can act confidently in serving God when we are moving in His will, sure of His faithfulness to confirm His Word by signs and wonders. Who would have thought that we would be delivered from discovery and probably arrest by a sudden thunderstorm or a dirty handkerchief?

The long flight across the Atlantic made for plenty of time to reminisce and to ponder the amazing things God had done over the years. I also began to wonder about what might happen now. Where would the next years lead me? How would I put into practice these lessons as I began the work for which God had created me? Which direction should I go from *ground zero?*

When I stepped off the plane and hurriedly walked to embrace Jan, Jill and Shane I was on my way to the greatest adventure of all: this thing called ministry.

Chapter X

Conclusion: No Greater Love

Normally the conclusion of a book represents the ending of the work, but for me it represents the beginning. No Greater Love Ministries was born in the Austrian Alps and began to take shape in 1975. During the eighties No Greater Love grew in many ways and continued to look to Christ for the power to be effective in ministry. Today, No Greater Love is actively pursuing our mission of "putting the gospel in the hands of faithful men." We take people from all walks of life and involve them in the ministry of evangelism on the streets of the United States, as well as internationally. These people, leaders of their local churches and young believers alike, all come to us with the hope of being used by God in communicating His gospel. They also come to learn from each other and to gain insights for effectively leading the churches and local ministries from which they come. The principles learned at every step along the road to *ground zero* continue to be guidelines for the everyday operation of our ministry and are important parts of our training throughout the world.

In the next chapter we hope to include you and to aid you in your own search for *ground zero*. In accordance with the Great Commission, No Greater Love does ministry locally, nationally and internationally. No Greater Love encourages individuals to take the same approach in ministry. Be involved in your local community, work and give to see your nation won to Christ and prayerfully work to take God's Word to other countries of the world.

No Greater Love offers each individual an opportunity to find the place God wants him to be. Your participation would fulfill our mission of equipping faithful men to participate in the Kingdom of God. I often am asked specifically what it is that No Greater Love does. Perhaps I have unintentionally discovered the answer: we help people find their own *ground zeros.*

The Rev. Fred L. Bishop
No Greater Love Ministries
P.O. Box 263
DuQuoin, IL 62832